Close Reading in Elementary School

The Common Core State Standards encourage teachers to use close reading as a means to help students access complex text. Many literacy experts believe close reading has the power to create strong, independent readers, but what does that *really* mean, and how does it work in the classroom? This book is your must-have guide to getting started! It provides step-by-step strategies and scaffolds for teaching close reading and improving students' comprehension of complex texts. You will learn how to teach close reading based on text type, how to transition students through increasingly challenging texts, and how to use close reading as a springboard for close writes and close talks.

Special Features:

♦ An easy-to-use framework for creating a close reading lesson

♦ Close reading strategies for a variety of literary and informational subgenres

♦ Ideas for teaching close reading to meet specific comprehension objectives based on the Common Core, including analyzing text structure and evaluating argument

♦ Suggestions for helping students read with increased levels of rigor

♦ A clear explanation of what text complexity really means and how it varies by student

♦ Scaffolds to help students at all ability levels do a close reading

♦ Guidelines and procedures for close talks—purposeful, focused discussions about text

♦ Procedures for close writes that vary based on genre and student ability level

In addition, each chapter includes study guide questions to help you apply the ideas in the book to your own classroom. With this practical book, you will have all the tools you need to make close reading a reality!

Diana Sisson and **Betsy Sisson**, Ed.D.s., are educational consultants who work with schools and speak internationally on the topic of improving literacy. They are adjunct professors at Central Connecticut State University and the University of Saint Joseph.

Close Reading in Elementary School

Bringing Readers and Texts Together

Diana Sisson and
Betsy Sisson

Routledge
Taylor & Francis Group

NEW YORK AND LONDON

First published 2014
by Routledge
711 Third Avenue, New York, NY 10017

and by Routledge
2 Park Square, Milton Park, Abingdon, Oxon OX14 4RN

Routledge is an imprint of the Taylor & Francis Group,
an informa business

Library of Congress Cataloging in Publication Data
Sisson, Diana.
  Close reading in elementary school: bringing readers and
  texts together/by Dr. Diana Sisson and Dr. Betsy Sisson.
  pages cm
  Includes bibliographical references and index.
  1. Reading (Elementary). 2. Literacy. I. Sisson, Betsy. II. Title.
  LB1573.S559 2014
  372.4—dc23
  2013043927

ISBN: 978-0-415-74613-7 (hbk)
ISBN: 978-0-415-74614-4 (pbk)
ISBN: 978-1-315-79754-0 (ebk)

Typeset in Palatino and Stone Sans
by Florence Production Ltd, Stoodleigh, Devon, UK

To Dr. Susan Ferrell
for starting us on our own journey
of bringing readers and texts together

CONTENTS

Preface   xi
Meet the Authors   xiii

PART I   UNDERSTANDING CLOSE READING   1

1 Defining Complex Text in the Classroom   3
         Why Is Text Complexity a Significant Factor
              in Reading Instruction Today?   4
         Measuring Text Complexity   6
         The Essence of Text Complexity   16
         Chapter Summary   19
         Book Study: Reflection Questions   20

2 Close Reading: Historical Perspectives and
       Contemporary Practices   21
         Historical Context   21
         Close Reading Comes to American Classrooms   22
         Reader Response Theory   24
         The Return of Close Reading   26
         Chapter Summary   30
         Book Study: Reflection Questions   32

PART II   CLOSE READING IN THE CLASSROOM   33

3 An Overview of Close Reading Strategies   35
         Ten Steps to Creating a Close Reading Lesson   35
         Scaffold the Implementation   42
         Chapter Summary   45
         Book Study: Reflection Questions   47

4   Reading Across Literary and Informational Genres   49

       Literary Genres   50

       Informational Genres   62

       Chapter Summary   75

       Book Study: Reflection Questions   76

5   Reading for Specific Comprehension Objectives   77

       Standard 1—Reading for Details Using Both

          Literal and Inferential Understanding   80

       Standard 2—Theme/Main Idea and Summarization   82

       Standard 3—Narrative Elements   89

       Standard 4—Vocabulary   92

       Standard 5—Text Structure   94

       Standard 6—Point of View   98

       Standard 7—Diverse Text Formats and Media   102

       Standard 8—Evaluate Arguments in Text   104

       Standard 9—Comparing and Contrasting

          Multiple Texts   107

       Chapter Summary   107

       Book Study: Reflection Questions   109

6   Reading with Increasing Levels of Rigor   111

       Bloom's Taxonomy   112

       Webb's DOK Levels   117

       Comparing Bloom's Taxonomy and Webb's

          DOK Levels   122

       Differentiating Academic Rigor   123

       Chapter Summary   128

       Book Study: Reflection Questions   130

PART III   **LINKING CLOSE READING WITH CLOSE TALKS AND CLOSE WRITES**   **131**

7   Using Close Talks to Deepen Understanding   133

       The Power of Questioning   135

       Close Talks   135

       Preparing a Close Talk   140

Guidelines for Participating in a Close Talk   141
Close Talk Procedure   142
Close Talk Participation Rubric   142
Benefits of Close Talk   144
Chapter Summary   146
Book Study: Reflection Questions   147

8 Close Writes as a Springboard into Student-Generated
       Writing   149
Reading–Writing Connection   150
The Close Write Model   153
Chapter Summary   170
Book Study: Reflection Questions   171

References   173

PREFACE

We have always been avid readers and honestly could not imagine not reading everything and anything . . . every day. When we were completing our undergraduate degree in elementary education, we were meeting with our academic advisor, and she asked if we had thought of studying reading education for our graduate work. Just like that—a light bulb went off, and we realized what better calling than to work with children who may never have experienced the joy of reading. It was not a hard decision to make.

We enrolled in that graduate program and have never looked back. While we have taken a variety of different positions, they have all shared one commonality—our focus to bring readers and texts together. We want every child to look at books as treats to enjoy, as a source of friendship, and as a way to learn more about the world around them.

Too often reading becomes an arduous chore for many and a source of anxiety and dread for others. Reading cannot be equated with worksheets and tests. Unfortunately, we in the education field often feel compelled to push students as quickly as possible through the content. Who hasn't said at some point, "I covered it. I don't know why they didn't learn it." That feeling and the actions that it triggers is what we would like to end.

Students need time to construct meaning from text, to re-read purposefully as they search for deeper understanding, and to think more reflectively about how the text is structured, what it truly means, and what they can learn about themselves as readers, writers, and thinkers. This kind of time requires us to plan intentionally. . .to provide the time they need to do this, to support them in this journey, and to offer them the tools they need to become not just good readers, not just great readers—but independent readers who feel confident when confronted with complex, challenging text.

The best way we know to accomplish all of these lofty goals is through the instructional practice of close reading. It is not a new concept. People have been reading closely for centuries beginning with the study of sacred texts across a variety of religious faiths. Since the 1920s, that drive to delve deeply into text has migrated to the academic world. While it originally entered American classrooms in the 1930s and 1940s, close reading has made a significant resurgence. Today, we once again look at close reading to help students approach text not as decoders but as analysts and evaluators. We ask students to read, to read again and again as they become active and engaged in the reading process.

There is a lot of work to be done to ensure that our students become the readers they need to be. Close reading can help make that happen. In this book, you will learn how to assess what makes a text complex and how that complexity is not constant but changing based on each unique reader who approaches it. We will trace the history of close reading to discover its beginnings as well as its influence in today's classrooms. We will also share practical applications of close reading as a means to teach comprehension using authentic, quality literature, to experience genres across literary and informational texts, and to raise academic rigor so that all students grow at their pace in a supportive environment. With all of that in place, we will demonstrate how close reading can lend its instructional strength to help students make their thinking visible—first through close talks and sustained class discussions about challenging content and then through close writes as a scaffold for students to learn how to be writers from mentor texts and from their own analysis of what effective writing looks like.

As you can see, close reading has the potential to transform your classroom and your instruction. All you need to do is turn the page and start on not just your own journey but that of your students . . . to bring readers and texts together.

MEET THE AUTHORS

Diana Sisson and Betsy Sisson, Ed.D.s., hold doctorates in Educational Leadership and Policy Studies as well as being certified reading consultants with a combined experience of over thirty years. The sisters have worked abroad in developing reading programs for students in international settings, consulted on federal research grants, presented at national and international conferences, and guest lectured at a number of universities. They currently work as reading consultants, serve as adjunct professors at Central Connecticut State University and the University of Saint Joseph in literacy, special education, and educational research as well as operate their own consulting company focusing on school improvement and professional development services.

Their professional publications center on equitable educational opportunities for all students. In addition to this book, they have written two others texts: *Targeted Reading Interventions for the Common Core Classroom—Tested Lessons That Help Struggling Students Meet the Rigors of the Standards—K-3* and *Targeted Reading Interventions for the Common Core Classroom—Tested Lessons That Help Struggling Students Meet the Rigors of the Standards—4 and Up.*

Diana and Betsy also sit on several International Reading Association committees and on the board of the Connecticut Association for Reading Research (CARR). In their capacity as research chairs for CARR, they are currently undertaking a study delving into teacher preparation programs in the field of literacy.

Part I

Understanding Close Reading

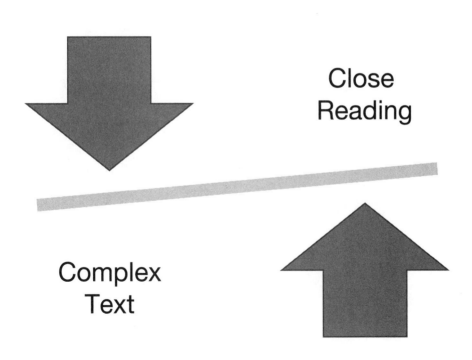

Close
Reading

Complex
Text

Defining Complex Text
in the Classroom

Can you predict whether a student will be a struggling reader, a strong reader, an excellent reader? How do you plan instruction to ensure that your students will be prepared to face the daily challenges of new and difficult text? Would you focus primarily on vocabulary or perhaps on developing comprehension skills? The reality is that students' ability to access challenging text has become the crossroads of literacy instruction. In effect, the skills needed to construct meaning from complex text become the gap that many readers cannot cross.

The goal of reading instruction is to teach students to construct meaning from text, and student ability—or inability—to construct meaning from challenging text is a key predictor of later achievement. This process begins with building the foundations of literacy, such as phonemic analysis and decoding. Students also learn to make surface-level meaning as well as to dig deeper to grasp inferential understanding. Although all of these skills are, unquestionably, critical to developing strong reading skills, as students encounter increasingly more sophisticated and content-driven texts they are compelled to process their learning at ever-deepening levels of complexity and simply cannot navigate through them without teacher support. Thus, the reading skills students acquire may be inhibited by texts that demand more resources than they can marshal, leaving students to flounder in the face of challenging material.

Complex text does not represent any new phenomenon in classrooms. Readers have struggled with difficult and "unfriendly" texts since the dawn of the printed word. What has changed is the sheer quantity of this material as well as rising expectations for their inclusion in classrooms. The days of Dick and Jane have been eclipsed by sophisticated picture books, the emphasis of nonfiction in primary grades, escalating Lexile ranges, and the demands of high-stakes standardized tests. What does this mean for today's classrooms? Complex text has vaulted into the national spotlight as a necessity for classroom instruction.

Why Is Text Complexity a Significant Factor in Reading Instruction Today?

Reading skills develop most appreciably in the primary grades and then slow down in the later grades. This simple fact has significant implications. First, developing foundational skills—including the ability to access difficult text—must be a strategic element of literacy instruction.

"A person who is not at least a modestly skilled reader by the end of third grade is quite unlikely to graduate from high school." (Snow, Burns, & Griffin, 1998, p. 21)

In order to increase skills and learn how to approach difficult text, students should begin in kindergarten rather than waiting until upper elementary and middle school when they have little or no experience in how to extract meaning from demanding passages. Second, lacking these skills can intensify the reading deficiencies already present in some young readers so that they stagnate at a given reading level and are unable to move forward into more demanding text. Third, as students transition from third to fourth grade, the well-known adage sets in—students learn to read by grade three and read to learn in fourth grade and beyond. Students also see a surge in content expectations. Without established skills in eliciting understanding from these specialized texts, they will falter in the upper grades. Fourth, this weakness in constructing meaning from what in the upper grades may be characterized as academically-driven, abstract, and dense texts, has grave repercussions on student learning outcomes later in their academic career. Fifth, the information age that has exploded in the last several years has created new expectations as "the sheer magnitude of human knowledge, globalization, and the accelerating rate of change due to technology necessitates a shift in our children's education—from plateaus of knowing to continuous cycles of learning" (North Central Regional Educational Laboratory and Metiri Group, 2003, p. 5).

Biancarosa and Snow (2004) found that about 8 million students in grades 4–12 struggle to read at grade level with approximately 70 percent of older readers needing remediation. *Education Week* reported in 2010 that 1.3 million students drop out of school annually or—even more staggering—over 7,000 students a day (Swanson, 2010). Researchers investigating this crisis have discovered that the most common reason students cite for their decision is their own perceived lack of literacy skills.

"Performance on complex texts is the clearest differentiator in reading between students who are likely to be ready for college and those who are not." (ACT, 2006, pp. 16–17)

The American Diploma Project (2004) studied the status of students who do graduate with a diploma from American high schools and formed the following conclusions:

♦ The majority of high school graduates require some form of remediation in postsecondary education.

♦ A significant number of university students never earn a degree.

♦ The majority of the business sector believes that high school graduates lack basic skills.

♦ Most high school graduates question the education they received to prepare them for the workforce.

Students who earn a high school diploma, then, have two options—seek postsecondary education or join the work force. In

2006, *Reading Between the Lines: What the ACT Reveals About College Readiness in Reading,* studied the 2005 results of high school graduates tested through *ACT.* Their findings reflected a serious deficit in reading skills: 49 percent of students tested were not prepared for college-level reading, and college-level readiness had already reached a decade-long decline. This academic deficit may account for the 46 percent of enrolled students who fail to earn an undergraduate degree after six years, roughly translating to 37 million Americans who have some postsecondary experience—but no degree (Cowan & Kessler, 2013). Of interest, the authors stated, "performance on complex texts is the clearest differentiator in reading between students who are likely to be ready for college and those who are not" (ACT, 2006, pp. 16–17).

These dire statistics are repeated in the American job market. In 2011, the report, *Boiling Point: The Skills Gaps in U. S. Manufacturing,* disclosed that with over 600,000 jobs open in the field, 67 percent of the respondents in their study reported a shortage of qualified workers and cited deficiencies in literacy skills as one of the contributing factors (Deloitte, 2011).

Taken together, research indicates that literacy instruction must not only encompass the traditional foundational skills of vocabulary and comprehension but also—and more significantly—the skill set needed to access and construct meaning from complex text. The ramifications of these skills, or the lack of them, will influence student achievement in the elementary grades and beyond.

Measuring Text Complexity

"Not only do strong skills drive high achievement in literacy, but they facilitate high achievement in math and science, too, where students often must read complex material to solve problems." (Gewertz, 2013, p. 9)

Professionals in the field of education have measured text complexity for nearly a century. It began with methods that allowed for quantifiable data to describe the relative sophistication and grade-appropriate levels (e.g., using readability formulas to determine grade-level approximations) and then progressed to qualitative study, relying on the expertise of the text analyst (e.g., reflecting on the relative complexity among literary genres, such as between science fiction and fairy tales). Today, it is possible to consider a range of quantitative and qualitative indicators, including that of the reader within the complexity equation (e.g., the reader's prior knowledge, motivation, or interest in the text).

Text Complexity through the Lens of Quantitative Indicators

Quantitative analysis of texts can be traced back to 1847 with the advent of the graded school in Boston. As students moved into grade-level classrooms, educators developed readability formulas in order to provide grade-level materials. These formulas furnished educators with the ability to use mathematical formulas to label texts appropriate for certain grade levels or age levels.

The first nationally-recognized readability formula was designed by Edward Thorndike in 1921 with his seminal work that applied the frequency of difficult words as a model for determining readability. Rudolph Flesch later developed one of the most popular readability formulas, the Flesch-Kincaid Grade Level, in which he calculated the number of syllables (semantic indicators) and the number of sentences (syntactic indicators) within a 100-word passage to analyze texts. In 1963, Fry transitioned from the use of formulas and manual calculations to his Fry Readability Graph, which facilitated the determination of grade-level estimates. That same year, computerized readability software appeared, which further eased the readability measures. Today, readability formulas have proliferated in the field with over 200 formulas currently available for educators to use when assessing students (see examples in Figure 1.1).

Although readability formulas benefit from objective, quantitative analysis, they have also generated controversy in the field. In 1981, the International Reading Association and the National Council of Teachers of English jointly cautioned against their use. Later, the College Entrance Examination Board also decried their ability to measure a text's relative readability accurately, electing to end their application as a means to measure college applicants' reading abilities.

- www.readability-score.com
- www.readabilityformulas.com/free-readability-formula-tests.php
- www.gunning-fog-index.com
- www.readabilityformulas.com/free-fry-graph-test.php
- www.lexile.com (Specializes in Lexile levels)
- www.read-able.com (Specializes in analysis of website texts)

Figure 1.1 Readability Formula Websites

This criticism stems from several concerns. A central argument emerges from whether or not to accept that the number of syllables and the number of words within a sentence truly captures a text's readability. In effect, does the number of syllables in a word dictate how challenging the word may be to the reader? Take for example the words *elephant* and *pachyderm*. Both contain three syllables. Both refer to the same animal. Are they equally challenging? Elementary students would definitely recognize the word elephant as well as possess a vivid mental image of what the animal looks like; few would have an equal mastery of pachyderm. This example illustrates the belief that quantitative measures, such as readability formulas, can measure only the most surface-level characteristics of text without taking into account the effects of vocabulary selection, writing style, text coherence, etc.

Another criticism is the notion that smaller sentences inherently create more "readable" text. Can shorter text guarantee higher comprehension? Neither can readability formulas consider the repetition of academic-domain words. While these words may be beyond the reader's experience, each repetition of these words adds to the reader's facility in using them. The formulas' accuracy must also be viewed through the variations in complexity, as books often flow among different readability levels throughout the text. If analyzed at the beginning of a book, for example, the measurement may indicate a lower readability than if the measurement was conducted in the middle or at the end of the text (Hiebert, 2011).

It has also further been established that readability formulas provide merely rough estimates of a text's readability. Some estimates place them at 80 percent accuracy while others focus on grade-level approximations, suggesting that the readability formula may be skewed by up to one year below or above its measurement.

Quantitative indicators, then, provide a truly objective analysis of the text based on the parameters set, in many cases, within the context of counting syllables and words in sentences. They also offer convenience as text can be measured through software—many of which can be found online at no cost. They do, however, suffer from inherent inaccuracies as well as the ongoing disagreement of their premise of how readability should be measured. In response to these concerns, qualitative indicators have emerged that offer cues for educators to review text and base complexity on their own professional opinion.

Text Complexity through the Lens of Qualitative Indicators

Anderson and Armbruster (1984) considered the characteristics of "considerate" texts and argued that "the research on the impact of text variables on comprehension and retention of text has not produced a coherent theoretical model" (p. 39) but advocated for indicators that included text structure, coherence, unity, and audience appropriateness (1984a). Despite writing about their concept of considerate texts, they ultimately advised against texts that are "ideal," seeming to be the harbinger for the text complexity issues currently facing students today.

The 2006 ACT report, *Reading Between the Lines: What the ACT Reveals About College Readiness*, suggested purely qualitative indicators for text complexity, including *relationships* (e.g., among ideas and characters), *richness* (e.g., level of

> "Are ideal texts desirable? Do they or could they lead to an attitude among readers that texts must come to the readers, and that if comprehension fails, it is the fault of the text? Is it possible for us to do too much for the reader? Comprehending and learning in the final analysis are carried out by the readers." (Anderson & Armbruster, 1984, p. 47)

sophistication in the transmission of information), *structure* (e.g., text structure), *style* (e.g., tone and language use), *vocabulary* (e.g., word choice), and *purpose* (e.g., author's intent). This model emphasizes the qualitative aspects of analyzing the degree of rigor of texts along a continuum of "uncomplicated," "more challenging," and "complex." For example, an uncomplicated purpose would be explicitly stated. A more challenging purpose would be expressed but with a certain degree of subtlety, and the complex purpose may be identified through implicit modes.

Fisher, Frey, and Lapp (2012) developed a rubric based on the work of the Common Core State Standards. In their model, they designate text complexity into three categories: comfortable, grade level, and a stretch. Their indicators include *density and complexity* (e.g., literal, multiple, or ambiguous meanings), *figurative language* (e.g., irony and symbolism), *purpose* (e.g., explicit, implicit, or deliberately withheld), *genre* (e.g., familiar, unfamiliar, or not adhering to parameters of a given genre), *organization* (e.g., conventional versus unconventional), *narration* (e.g., credible voice, limited perspective, or unreliable voice), *text features and graphics* (e.g., clearly organized information to limited use of graphics), *standard English and variations* (e.g., text that aligns closely to the reader's linguistic basis versus variations of standard English not familiar to the reader), *register* (e.g., casual, formal, or archaic in a domain-specific scholarly style), *background knowledge* (e.g., focusing on reader's personal experiences), *prior knowledge* (e.g., focusing on academic learning), *cultural knowledge* (e.g., centers on familiar cultural templates versus text characterized by outdated or historical cultures), and *vocabulary* (e.g., controlled, domain specific, and delineated by complex ideas with few context clues to support reading).

Hess & Hervey (2010, updated 2011) also developed a rubric stemming from the work of Common Core State Standards. This model specified text complexity into four categories ranging from simple texts to very complex texts. Its indicators comprised the *length of the text, format and layout of text, genre, level of meaning and reasoning required by the reader* (e.g., explicit versus implied purpose), *text structure and discourse style* (e.g., irony and satire), *words, language features,* and *structure* (e.g., Tier II words versus Tier III words), and *background knowledge demands.*

What all of these models of qualitative indicators share are twofold. First, they emphasize a deeper, more sophisticated scrutiny of the text considering its meaning and structure over that of the quantitative indicators of words (semantics) and sentences (syntax). Second, they depict the complexity more accurately when used in conjunction with quantitative indicators. This interdependence was captured by the architects of the Common Core State Standards (CCSS) when they elected to merge the two into a holistic approach to measuring text complexity.

Text Complexity through the CCSS Blending of Quantitative and Qualitative Indicators

The Common Core State Standards utilized a triangle model with three primary components: quantitative aspects, qualitative aspects, and reader and task aspects (National Governors Association Center for Best Practices and the Council of Chief State School Officers, 2010). Using this standard, they merged quantitative and qualitative indicators while also emphasizing the importance of the reader (see Figure 1.2).

CCSS Quantitative Indicators. Each textual aspect has significant bearing on a reader's ability to determine meaning. Quantitative indicators encompass a range of text parameters—all of which can be measured in some way. Because of its numerical results, quantitative analysis presents the most easily identifiable rating of how rigorous the reading expectation may be. Within this category, it refers to "text complexity, such as word length or frequency, sentence length, and text cohesion, that are difficult if not impossible for a human reader to evaluate efficiently, especially in long texts, and are thus today typically measured by computer software" (National Governors Association Center for Best Practices and the Council of Chief State School Officers, 2010, p. 4).

Word length. An initial step in determining the complexity of text resides in the difficulty of its words. Words of one or two syllables are inherently less difficult to read than those of three, four, or five

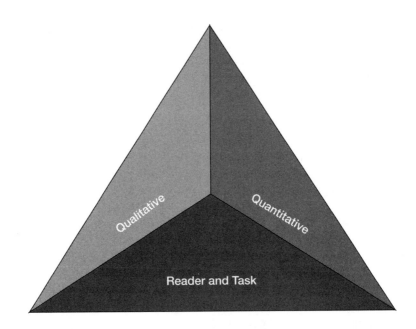

Figure 1.2 Dimension of Text Complexity

Note: From *Common Core State Standards for English language arts and literacy in history/social studies, science, and technical subjects. Appendix A: Supporting key elements of the standards and glossary of key terms* (p. 4), by National Governors Association Center for Best Practices & Council of Chief State School Officers, 2010. Washington, DC: Authors. Copyright 2010 by the National Governors Association Center for Best Practices and the Council of Chief State School Officers. All rights reserved.

syllables. It does, however, necessitate more than a cursory look at the passage. For example, as discussed previously, elephant and pachyderm both contain three syllables and are, in fact, used to indicate the same animal. Despite this, their relative difficulty is vastly different. An elementary student would be expected to recognize and understand the word elephant. That expectation would not hold for pachyderm.

Word frequency. Word frequency focuses on vocabulary—a primary indicator for challenging text. "The word frequency measure gives a sense of how many rare words are in a text. Rare words are ones that occur once or a few times for every million words of text" (Hiebert, 2012, n.p.). The greater presence of rare words, the greater the text complexity. Likewise, fewer rare words denote less text complexity. A simple method to define what constitutes a rare word may be borrowed from the work of Isabel Beck and her classification of vocabulary into three distinct tiers. Tier I words reflect basic, concrete words. Tier II words refer to general academic words frequently encountered in text, and Tier III words signify domain-specific words and phrases essential for content-area study. Using this classification system, rare words may occasionally materialize from Tier II but would most often occur at the Tier III level. How significant are rare words?

> An increase of only one or two percent in rare vocabulary can make texts considerably more complex. When viewed from the vantage point of a thousand-word text, a rate of 8% means the text has about 80 rare words, while a rate of 10% means that a text has about 100 rare words. An additional two rare words in every 100 words can increase the challenge of a text.
>
> (Hiebert, 2013, p. 2)

Sentence length. The length of the sentence influences the reader's ability to access the text, in that shorter sentences require less cognitive resources than do longer sentences, freeing the brain to focus on sentence-level, paragraph-level, and passage-level meaning and not on word-by-word meaning. Longer sentences tend to be more sophisticated with a greater range of sentence variety, which the reader must recognize and interpret for meaning.

Text cohesion. Texts are commonly classified as coherent at the "local" level or the "global level." Typified by their ability to fit together, the local level occurs within small pieces of a text, such as at the paragraph level. Conversely, the global level refers to text portions longer than a paragraph (Groen, 1996). McCrimmon (as cited in Bamberg, 1983) defined a paragraph as being coherent when "the reader can move easily from one sentence to the next and read the paragraph as an integrated whole, rather than a series of separate sentences" (p. 417). Thus, the ease with which a reader can move through text may, in part, derive from the capacity for sentences and paragraphs to flow together as a cohesive unit of thoughts and ideas.

CCSS Qualitative Indicators. Qualitative aspects refer to "text complexity best measured or only measurable by an attentive human reader, such as: levels of meaning or purpose; structure; language conventionality and clarity; and knowledge demands" (National Governors Association Center for Best Practices and the Council of Chief State School Officers, 2010, p. 4). It also encompasses a range of issues, including those highlighted below.

Genre. The genre can greatly influence the level of understanding needed to approach the text. For example, a fairy tale with the sheer predictability of characters and plot development is vastly easier to understand than the inherently surprising and unexpected narrative found in science fiction. Likewise, in nonfiction, the clearly-delineated narrative flow characteristic of biography is more accessible than that of the twists and turns associated with science fiction.

Writing style. The way in which an author writes can influence the ability of a reader to construct meaning. Elements of an author's writing style encompass word choice, sentence structure and fluency, formal versus informal voice, etc. How these elements converge results in a measure of readability.

Sentence/text complexity. In the early primary grades, text usually comprises short sentences with a simple subject and predicate. Sentence complexity grows, however, to incorporate compound sentences, complex sentences, compound-complex sentences, etc. This variety of sentence structure represents not only the potential increase of content rigor but also the very real increase of sentence by sentence complexity as each of these structures requires a deeper understanding of English syntax and a corresponding greater need for cognitive resources to process the thoughts and ideas expressed by the author.

Non-literal language. Elementary students process information primarily through literal meanings, commonly struggling to grasp the true meaning of non-literal or figurative language. Non-literal language includes alliteration, hyperbole, idioms, imagery, meta-phors, onomatopoeia, personification, and similes. In the case of idiomatic language alone, its prevalence in the English language has far-reaching implications. A seminal study in 1977 found that within 200,000 oral (i.e., speeches and dialogues) and written words (i.e., adult and student-generated compositions) analyzed in documents, idioms appeared at an average rate of 4.08 per minute (Pollio, Barlow, Fine, & Pollio, 1977). A later study conducted by Cooper in 1998 examined television programs and other forms of oral communication revealed that people used between three and four idiomatic expressions per minute—often crucial to constructing meaning from the content. Readers who lack experience with non-literal language will thus find themselves at a disadvantage.

Explicit versus implicit themes and ideas. Themes and ideas expressed explicitly demands less of a reader's cognitive resources than that required by text written in a much more implicit style. For example, when forming the foundations for the concept of theme to primary students, fables provide a clear story lesson.

CCSS Reading and Task Indicators. Reader and task aspects suggests that "while the prior two elements of the model focus on the inherent complexity of text, variables specific to particular readers (such as motivation, knowledge, and experiences) and to particular tasks (such as purpose and the complexity of the task assigned and the questions posed) must also be considered when determining whether a text is appropriate for a given student" (National Governors Association Center for Best Practices and the Council of Chief State School Officers, 2010, p. 4).

Background knowledge. Prior Knowledge. Schema. All of these terms describe the experiences a reader has with content prior to reading. Essentially, background knowledge is "what one already knows about a subject" (Stevens, 1980, p. 151). It reflects what the reader brings to the text to aid in comprehension. Marzano (2004), in fact, suggests that it is prior knowledge of the content that will ultimately provide the most significant indicator of students' ability to acquire new learning.

Student interest in topic. In addition to past experiences, the reader's personal interest in a topic also affects text complexity. For example, the level of complexity for texts that encompasses topics in which students are interested naturally decreases; on the other hand, texts on topics of little or no interest to students increase in complexity. For example, consider the Harry Potter series of J. K. Rowling. Although the text was quantitatively complex, many young readers happily tackled it.

Student motivation. Motivation, although often overlooked in the equation of how readers construct meaning, remains a key component of what can make a text complex, or not. Cambria and Guthrie (2010) argue

> There are two sides to reading. On one side are the skills which include phonemic awareness, phonics, word recognition, vocabulary, and simple comprehension. On the other side is the will to read. A good reader has both skill and will. In the "will" part, we are talking about motivation to read. This describes children's enjoyments, their wants, and their behaviors surrounding reading. A student with skill may be capable, but without will, she cannot become a reader.
>
> (p. 16)

The motivation, or engagement, that a reader brings to the reading process has profound influence on the perceived difficulty of text. Students' self-perceptions about their reading and their interest in the activity patently shape their ability to construct meaning.

Achieve the Core (2013) recommends the use of all three indicators as a means to place books at the appropriate grade level. First, use the quantitative measures to determine the grade-level band of the text. Then, implement the qualitative measures to place the text within the grade-level band. Hiebert (2011) stresses that "once quantitative data establish that particular texts are 'within the ballpark,' the hard work of qualitative analyzing the demands of texts in relation to different readers and tasks begin" (pp. 2–3). Finally, review the text using professional judgment to determine how appropriate the text is for the instructional purpose and students.

The Essence of Text Complexity

In determining the complexity of text, it is possible to consider quantitative factors or qualitative factors. If either choice is selected, it should be understood that the true indicator of whether a text may prove difficult lays not solely in counting syllables and sentences or the writing style of the author. *The reader—not the text—ultimately determines text complexity.* What is complex to one is not complex to another (see Figure 1.3).

Being aware of the inherent importance of the student in the text complexity equation compels educators to reflect on instructional practice in two strategic ways. First, a common text may not be difficult for all students. So, it will be important to consider if conducting a close reading will be worthy of the time and effort for all students. Second, it will be easier to facilitate student construction

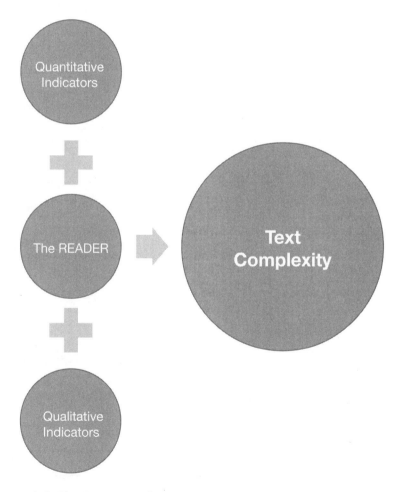

Figure 1.3 The Text Complexity Equation

of meaning by analyzing which aspect (quantitative, qualitative, or reader/task) is influencing its accessibility to the student.

The Text Complexity Checklist in Figure 1.4 provides an evaluative tool to analyze text as a means to measure its relative level of difficulty for students and its appropriateness in classroom instruction. It should also guide the selection process for those texts necessitating close reading lessons. Each item "checked" as characteristic of the text indicates increasing degrees of challenge for readers. As a rule of thumb, four or more checked items suggest a text that may be considered as complex.

	TEXT CHARACTERISTIC
Quantitative Indictors	Word Length Does the text contain more multisyllabic than monosyllabic words?
	Word Frequency Are rare words used within the text?
	Sentence Length Is the majority of sentences long?
Qualitative Indicators	Text Structure Is the text structure sophisticated, e.g., problem/solution?
	Text Features and Graphics Does the text lack text supports (e.g., headings, subheadings, vocabulary words in bold, glossary) and graphics/illustrations to aid comprehension?
	Sentence Complexity Are complex sentence structures frequently used in the text?
	Non-Literal Language Does the text contain multiple examples of non-literal language?
Reader Indicators	Background Knowledge Does the text demand previous prior knowledge or content knowledge in order to construct meaning?
	Student Interest Does the topic hold little interest for the reader?
	Motivation Does the student demonstrate little "will" to read the text?

Figure 1.4 Text Complexity Checklist

Chapter Summary

Text complexity has moved to the forefront of the educational field as an integral component of effective literacy instruction. Students who lack the ability to access challenging material are at a distinct disadvantage not only in reading but also in content area subjects, and this barrier will influence their academic achievement well beyond the elementary grades.

Measuring text complexity initially derived from the efforts of quantitative analysis, specifically in the work of readability formulas. First developed in response to graded schools where educators needed to provide grade-level appropriate texts, they soon became popular for their objective evaluation of instructional materials. They do, however, have critics who suggest that utilizing a formula constituted of length of words (semantics) and length of sentences (syntax) does not accurately determine readability. Their detractors also disparage formulas' accuracy based on a number of other issues, including the lack of attention to the repetition of rare and academic-domain vocabulary, and the variation of readability levels throughout a given text.

Qualitative indicators have been developed over the course of the last few decades in which literacy experts have argued their superiority over the previously preferred quantitative indicators. Common markers for qualitative analysis encompass author's writing style and word choice, genre and text features, and the explicit versus implicit demonstration of themes and ideas presented in the text.

Architects of the Common Core State Standards elected to merge these indicators with an addition of the reader/task aspects. The reader/task indicators focus on background knowledge, reader interest, and reader motivation.

While all of these indicators are undeniably important in measuring text complexity, the most essential gauge is that of the reader. Beyond all of the quantitative and qualitative criteria, it is the reader who ultimately determines what is complex, and this measure is unique and personal to each reader.

Book Study

Reflection Questions

Chapter 1: Defining Complex Text in the Classroom

1. What is complex text?

2. Do you believe that text complexity affects student achievement? Why or why not?

3. What do you believe to be the best measures for complex text (i.e., quantitative, qualitative, or reader/task)? What makes this indicator more accurate than the other two?

4. Does "complexity" change for different students? How?

5. How do you help students to access complex text in your classroom?

6. *TASK*: Select a text from your classroom. Working collaboratively with a colleague, analyze it for text complexity. Were you surprised by the results?

2

Close Reading

Historical Perspectives and Contemporary Practices

Close reading is purposeful re-readings and analysis of short pieces of complex text. With a clear instructional purpose set for the close reading of a passage, each reading, or *reading cycle*, centers on a question or task that moves the student closer and closer to the instructional target. Each reading cycle and its accompanying question or task, then, must be intentional and progressive in its movement toward the ultimate purpose—so the individual reading cycles operate as discrete objectives while simultaneously advancing student thinking and understanding toward a predetermined goal.

Historical Context

Close reading can be traced to the term *exegesis*, which derives from the Greek, meaning to "lead out" and refers to the critical explanation or interpretation of a text, specifically sacred text (Juel, 1998; Spolsky, 1990). In 2009, Gorman

"If reading is to accomplish anything more than passing time, it must be active." (Adler, 1941, p. 11)

suggested that "another appropriate description of exegesis is 'close reading' a term borrowed from the study of literature" (p. 10).

From an academic setting, close reading emerged from the field of literary criticism and centered on the concept of interpreting text by reading closely and considering specific elements of the text, such as its structure, its syntax, word choice, etc. Within this academic context, I. A. Richards, a professor at Cambridge University, first brought the underlying theory to use in the 1920s. In his 1929 book, *Practical Criticism: A Study of Literary Judgment*, he suggested that one of the aims of his work was to "prepare the way for education methods more efficient than those we use now . . . to understand what we hear and read" (p. 3). In his book, he described how he gave his undergraduate students a series of poems with no identifying markers, such as titles, authors, or background information, and instructed the students to analyze these de-contextualized poems by focusing on "the words on the page" rather than any preconceived notions about them. After studying their written responses, he reported that they were unable to comment on the texts with any sense of precision or objectivity. Based on his observations, he advocated for a reading protocol that disregarded the author's intentions or the reader's reactions and, instead, focused on the text itself.

His most prominent student, Richard Empson, authored his own book in 1930 entitled *Seven Types of Ambiguity* in which he compiled his undergraduate work with Richards into a study of the complex meanings of poetry. His support of minute close reading of literary texts paved the way for a new approach to literary criticism in the United States.

Close Reading Comes to American Classrooms

His work was later published in the United States (Empson, 1947) and would lead to a novel methodology for literary criticism, which would become known as "New Criticism" in which advocates would argue for the absence of identifying markers in place of readers focusing their attention on a sustained, detailed analysis of text and what that text reveals through careful interpretation, asserting that text has meaning in and of itself. The term, New Criticism, derives from John Crowe Ransom's 1941 book, *The New Criticism*, which coalesced from his own teaching methods and proposed approaching texts as self-contained and self-referential. Consequently, advocates of this style of literary criticism, who would become known as New Critics, focused on a "close reading" of text, linking structure and meaning while divorcing themselves from the reader's reaction, the author's intent, or the context of the work (biographical, historical, or cultural). Centering on the intrinsic meaning contained in text rather than the extrinsic meaning created by authors and readers, they sought to make the reading of literature a scientific process with its own vocabulary, claiming that observing the literary conventions would lead to a deeper understanding of the text. This stance emphasized a linguistic analysis of such textual elements as plot, point of view, figurative language, imagery, etc., asserting that the best readers were those who could analyze a text through these constituent components. This methodology became pervasive not just in postsecondary education but also in American high schools and junior highs and could later be found in elementary school as well with their focus on literary conventions as a means to understand text.

Adler (1940), believing that few readers can read for deep understanding but were capable with appropriate instruction, suggested his own rendering of close attention to text. He defined the art of reading as

> the process whereby a mind, with nothing to operate on but the symbols of the readable matter, and no help from outside, elevates itself by the power of its own operations. The mind passes from understanding less to understanding more ... obviously it is a more active kind of reading ... obviously too, things that are usually regarded as more difficult to read ...
>
> (Adler & Van Doren, 1972, p. 8)

He reasoned that this style of reading should only be undertaken in the presence of two conditions. First, the text must first initially be misunderstood—outside the grasp of the reader. Second, the reader must be able to overcome this break in comprehension—thus, reaching the goal of communication between the text and the reader.

Within this focused reading, Adler (1941) also encouraged marking up the text, arguing that "reading, if it is active, is thinking, and thinking tends to express itself in words, spoken or written" (p. 11) and so set forth guidelines for marking the text, including underlining or highlighting (e.g., significant points), asterisks (e.g., most important statements), numbers in the margin (e.g., sequence of points), circling or highlighting (e.g., key phases), and writing in the margins (e.g., noting questions, summarizing).

Reader Response Theory

Contrasting the beliefs of the New Critics, Louise Rosenblatt's groundbreaking texts, *Literature as Exploration* (1938) and *The Reader, the Text, the Poem: The Transactional Theory of the Literary Work* (1978) argued that reading involves an interaction between the reader and the text. Diametrically opposite of New Criticism, which viewed the text as central to meaning and encouraged objective analysis, Rosenblatt's Transactional Theory, or Reader Response Theory, asserted that textual meaning derives from the interaction between the text and the reader. The text, she argued, has no meaning without the presence of the reader and what the reader brings to the text.

> The special meaning, and more particularly, the submerged associations that these words and images have for the individual reader will largely determine what the work communicates to him. The reader brings to the work personality traits, memories of past events, present needs and preoccupations, a particular mood of the moment, and a particular physical condition. These and many other elements in a never-to-be-duplicated combination determine his response to the peculiar contribution of the text.
>
> (Rosenblatt, 1938, pp. 30–31)

She further theorized that a reader has two potential stances, or attitudes, when approaching texts—aesthetic and efferent. In the aesthetic stance, the reader enjoys the text on a purely personal level. Conversely, an efferent stance applies more readily to informational text and ensures that "the primary concern of the reader is with what he will carry away from the reading" (Rosenblatt, 1978, p. 24). These two positions, she hypothesized, influence the reading experience as well as what meaning the reader will extract from the text—be it emotion (i.e., aesthetic) or fact (i.e., efferent). Consequently, the stance, or purpose, that the reader assumes when approaching the text determines, in great part, what the reader will ultimately take away from the experience (Paulson & Armstrong, 2010).

Rosenblatt's work swept through American classrooms, supplanting much of New Criticism literary theory (see Figure 2.1). Critics of reader response suggested that accepting varied meanings dependent upon the reader devalued the text, as readers cannot be reliable interpreters of text and to focus on the role of the reader blurs the distinction between the text and its readers. In fact, two primary principles held by New Critics were *intentional fallacy* and *affective fallacy*. This "intentional fallacy," they reasoned, occurred when the reader believes that the author's intent determined the meaning of the text. Similarly, an "affective fallacy" arises when the reader believes that the reader's response influences the meaning of the text.

Nevertheless, by the 1970s, Reader Response Theory had entered the domain of classroom instruction, linking with the Whole Language Movement as attention shifted from teacher-directed to student-centered (Goodman, 1989; Gutteridge, 2000; Harris & Hodges, 1995; Taylor, 2007). Likewise, classroom instruction shifted from text-dependent analysis toward incorporating making reader connections, predicting, visualizing, writing reader response essays, and keeping writing journals as a means for students to construct distinct, individual meanings of what they read. This transformation of how readers approach text occurred both in K-12 schools as well as in many colleges and universities (Flippo & Caverly, 2009; Goodman, 1989).

New Criticism	Reader Response
Text is central to meaning	There is no meaning in the absence of the reader; the reader brings meaning to text
Focuses on the text	Focuses on the role of the reader
Text is an independent entity	Text is dependent upon the reader
Meaning already exists within the text—it is waiting for the reader to discover it	Reader constructs the meaning of the text
Emphasizes structure, literary conventions, syntax, etc.	Emphasizes prior knowledge, feelings, emotions, and personal reactions
Analysis is objective and detached from reader emotion	Analysis is subjective and personal to the reader
Meaning is constant with a single, accurate interpretation	Meaning changes reader to reader and may change at different stages of life of an individual reader based on life experiences
Meaning is self-contained and intrinsic to the text	Meaning relies on the reader and is extrinsic to the text
Teacher directs student attention to answer specific comprehension questions	Reader offers a personal impression of the text
Close reading offers the pathway to finding the meaning of text	Reader response fosters students' personal experiences with the text in order to derive meaning

Figure 2.1 New Criticism Versus Reader Response Theory

The Return of Close Reading

This approach to reading instruction continued until 2010 when Common Core State Standards (National Governors Association Center for Best Practices and the Council of Chief State School Officers, 2010) burst onto the educational field. Returning to the reading philosophy of New Criticism, the architects of CCSS set in motion a dramatic shift in classrooms across the country (Calkins, Ehrenworth, & Lehman, 2012). They engineered a return to textual analysis and close reading, abandoning background knowledge, personal connections, and reader response.

Close reading figured prominently within the document. Anchor Standard 1 of the College and Career Readiness Anchor Standards for Reading stated that students should "read closely to determine what the text says explicitly and to make logical inferences from it" (National Governors Association Center for Best Practices and the Council of Chief State School Officers, 2010). Standard 10 asserted that students should "read and comprehend complex literary and informational texts independently and proficiently" and goes on to suggest that this standard will allow students to "acquire the habits of reading independently and closely, which are essential to their future success" (National Governors Association Center for Best Practices and the Council of Chief State School Officers, 2010, p. 10).

With these simple statements, the CCSS established an expectation for what reading instruction should look like in contemporary classrooms. More importantly, however, close reading provides an effective tool to support students as they encounter greater and greater amounts of complex text that dominates instructional materials as well as the diverse texts encountered daily in the technological world in which we now live. This sentiment can be found in the perspectives of various experts as they share their definitions of close reading and what they find to be particularly powerful about its use (see Figure 2.2). We believe that by using close reading as a systematic scaffold in your instruction—regardless of the expectations of CCSS—you will be helping to ensure that your students are not just good readers but independent readers.

This, then, is where we begin. So far, we have defined complex text and what it means for your students and for your instructional planning and delivery. We have traced the origins of close reading, how it has intertwined with reading instruction in the United States, and how today it has taken an unprecedented role in reading instruction. Now, it is time for us to get to work.

In Part II, we will show you how to introduce close reading in your classroom as well as give you a framework for close reading lessons. With the framework as a guide, we will go on to provide concrete examples for using close reading lessons to teach comprehension objectives, to teach varied genres, and to raise the academic rigor of your classroom.

Source	Quote	Emphasis
Gorman, M. J. (2009). *Elements of biblical exegesis: A basic guide for students and ministers.* Peabody, MA: Hendrickson Publishers.	"Close reading means the deliberate, word-by-word and phrase-by-phrase consideration of all parts of a text in order to understand it as a whole."	Looks at close reading through the lens of exegesis of sacred texts; focuses on the analytical aspect of close reading as the reader deconstructs the text as a means to look at its constituent parts to understand the text as a whole
Brummet, B. S. (2010). *Techniques of close reading.* Thousand Oaks, CA: Sage Publications.	Close reading involves "the mindful, disciplined reading of an object (i.e., text) with the view to a deeper understanding of its meanings."	Stresses the importance of text-dependent study of text
Partnership for Assessment of Readiness for College and Careers (2011). *PARCC model content frameworks: English language arts/literacy grades 3-11.* Retrieved from www. parcconline. org/sites/parcc/files/ PARCCMCFELA LiteracyAugust2012_ FINAL.pdf	"Close, analytic reading stresses engaging with a text of sufficient complexity directly and examining meaning thoroughly and methodically, encouraging students to read and re-read deliberately. Directing student attention on the text itself empowers students to understand the central ideas and key supporting details. It also enables students to reflect on the meanings of individual words and sentences; the order in which sentences unfold; and the development of ideas over the course of the text, which ultimately leads students to arrive at an understanding of the text as a whole."	Highlights the value of close reading for students
Coleman, D. (2011). *David Coleman: Common core: Summer 2011.* [Audio podcast]. Retrieved from	"[By teaching close reading] you are empowering [students] to independently read and gain knowledge . . . what I'm trying to do here which is to rehabilitate a	Underscores the need to focus on text to discover meaning as well as on the power of close reading in the reading lives of students

Figure 2.2 Perspectives on Close Reading

www.youtube.com/watch?v=aTCiQVCpdQc&feature=youtube	world in which the text plays a central role, where we acknowledge its confusions and gradually work through them, taking the time and care to linger, particularly where the author chooses to linger, letting them be our guide as to what questions are most interesting because that, of course, was their fundamental work."	
Brown, S., & Kappes, L. (2012). *Implementing the common core state standards: A primer on "close reading" of text*. Washington, DC: The Aspen Institute.	"Close reading of text involves an investigation of a short piece of text, with multiple readings done over multiple instructional lessons. Through text-based questions and discussion, students are guided to deeply analyze and appreciate various aspects of the text."	Underscores the teacher support needed throughout the close reading process
Fisher, D., Frey, N., & Lapp, D. (2012). *Text complexity: Raising rigor in reading*. Newark, DE: International Reading Association.	"Close reading is an instructional routine in which students critically examine a text, especially through repeated readings . . . Close reading invites students to examine the deep structures of a piece of text. . .these deep structures include the way the text is organized, the precision of its vocabulary to advance concepts, and its key details, arguments, and inferential meanings."	Accentuates the need to make close reading a habitual practice in classrooms
Shanahan, T. (2012, June 18). Re: *What is close reading?* [Web log message]. Retrieved from www.shanahanonliteracy.com/2012/06/what-is-close-reading.html	"Close reading is an intensive analysis of a text in order to come to terms with what it says, how it says it, and what it means."	Draws attention to how close reading can bring readers and texts together

Figure 2.2 *Continued*

We also want you to consider how close reading can, and should, be about more than just reading complex text. If used purposefully, it can provide a structure for academic discourse with your students, allowing them to benefit from the use of dialogue to solidify and to expand their content knowledge. It also has the capability to launch student writing by building off well-written passages as mentor texts. Part III, then, will demonstrate how "close talks" and "close writes" can follow the instructional guidelines of close reading with the focused intent of developing discourse and writing skills.

Chapter Summary

Close reading is purposeful re-readings and analysis of short pieces of complex text. Although it has become a widely-discussed technique in the educational field, it actually has roots in the reading of sacred texts, known as *exegesis*, spanning several centuries. By the 1920s, I. A. Richards, a Cambridge professor, brought the concept of reading texts closely and purposefully to literature. Soon after, a student of his, William Empson, wrote of his experiences with Richards and soon his work migrated to the United States where it continued to gain popularity and soon became a key tenet in the literary theory known as New Criticism.

New Criticism espouses that the text alone determines meaning— with the exclusion of the author's intent or the reader's reaction to it. Developed as a scientific approach to reading, it relied heavily on the structure of text, literary conventions (e.g., plot, point of view, figurative language), syntax, and other textual elements as the formula for discovering the meaning inherent in text as well as the structured use of close reading as a vehicle for delving deeply into text to analyze these component parts. Prevalent not only in postsecondary institutions, New Criticism found its way into American high schools and junior highs. The use of literary conventions also became a mainstay in the education of elementary students.

By the 1970s, New Criticism began to wane, and Louise Rosenblatt's Transactional Theory, or Reader Response Theory, offered an alternative view of the reading process. She argued that it is not the text that holds meaning; rather, it is the reader who brings meaning to text. Without the reader, she asserted, there is no meaning. In fact, she theorized that the meaning of text alters from reader to reader and, even, alters at different stages of a reader's life. As Reader Response Theory gained traction in classrooms, students were encouraged to make personal connections, to predict what may happen next in the narrative, to keep book logs, to write reader response essays, etc.

The arrival of Common Core State Standards shifted instruction back to the tenets of New Criticism with its adherence to text-dependent questioning and close reading to the exclusion of Reader Response Theory and its reading ideology. Once again, close reading has come to the foreground as the key to unlock text. It has arrived at a critical time as students face complex and sophisticated texts not just in classrooms but also in their daily interactions with digital text, mass media, and the ever-changing world around them. Text of all kinds is becoming more complex every day. Close reading provides a reliable method for students to examine these texts in meaningful ways.

Book Study

Reflection Questions

*Chapter 2: Close Reading: Historical Perspectives
and Contemporary Practices*

1. What are the origins of close reading?

2. What elements of New Criticism do you see in your classroom?

3. Why do you think that instructional approaches (e.g., New Criticism and Reader Response Theory) change? Are they an indication of student performance or changing cultural times or something else?

4. What advantages and disadvantages do you see in New Criticism? Reader Response Theory?

5. How do you envision integrating close reading into your instructional practice?

6. *TASK*: Imagine a lesson you will soon be teaching. How would you structure it if you aligned it to New Criticism? How would it differ if you adhered to Reader Response Theory? Which one do you believe is the most effective with your students?

Part II

Close Reading in the Classroom

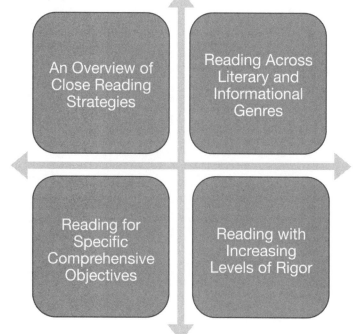

An Overview of Close Reading Strategies

Reading Across Literary and Informational Genres

Reading for Specific Comprehensive Objectives

Reading with Increasing Levels of Rigor

An Overview of
Close Reading Strategies

Instituting close reading strategies into classroom instruction can be challenging—both for you and for your students. In your case, you may not yet be comfortable with when, where, and why you want to utilize close reading strategies. For students, they rarely want to re-read a text so the challenge is how to engage them in the text and ensure that each of their readings further their understanding of the content. One of the best ways to make that happen is for you to learn the framework for conducting a close reading lesson and then facilitate your students' exposure to challenging content in a safe, supportive environment as they learn how revisiting text can help them be better readers.

Ten Steps to Creating a Close Reading Lesson

There are ten easy steps to develop a well-designed lesson incorporating close reading strategies. Utilizing the framework in your classroom builds a foundation for your students as they grapple with the ongoing demands of challenging text.

CLOSE READING FRAMEWORK

Step 1:   Identify the text.

Step 2:   Determine purpose for reading.

Step 3:   Choose a model.

Step 4:   Decide how students will access texts.

Step 5:   Complete first cycle of reading and present question/task.

Step 6:   Provide time for discussion.

Step 7:   Complete second cycle of reading and present question/task.

Step 8:   Provide time for discussion.

Step 9:   Complete third cycle of reading and present question/task.

Step 10: Provide time for discussion.

Step 1: Identify the Text. The most important step is the first—select the text. Close reading strategies should not be done with every reading nor should it be used every day. These strategies are designed for those texts that necessitate instructional support and extended time for students to analyze the text, absorb its intent, and reflect on its meaning. Thus, identifying the text becomes crucial in its effectiveness in your classroom.

In addition, students are focusing on only one passage, perhaps even a paragraph or two, of a larger text so you must also decide what piece of your identified text you believe will be the most challenging to your students. Remember that you shouldn't conduct a close reading on an entire book (unless it is a picture book) or an entire chapter. You are focusing on one key passage that promises to be the most problematic for your students and, yet, may be the key to unlocking the content for them.

So, don't conduct a close reading activity for a piece of text unless you believe that without these strategies, students will struggle and may fail to understand the content. Use the checklist in Figure 3.1 to help you make that determination.

Is the text truly challenging? Remember to consider the quantitative, qualitative, and reader and task aspects to make your decision (see Chapter 1). *Will it require re-reading*? Texts that are complex will compel students to peel away layers of meaning to come to a full understanding. Think about it in the context of the levels of reading comprehension, as shown in Figure 3.2. The first layer is literal comprehension. Your students may read the passage the first time to grasp only what is directly stated by the author, i.e., surface comprehension. After the second cycle of reading, you will focus on inferential comprehension to help them understand what the intent is for the passage, i.e., intermediate comprehension. Finally, you will ask your students to read again, and this time they may delve into the third level of comprehension—the evaluative level, i.e., core comprehension. After these multiple readings, students will use the previous two layers to help them create informed judgments about the text.

Does the text need to be chunked? Will breaking the text apart help your students access it easier and have greater opportunities to interpret it? Of equal importance, is this passage the key to unlocking the content for them? *Will classroom discussion help your students to process the content*? One of the central features of a close reading activity is the time you devote to students talking with you and with their classmates. As a means of making thinking visible, public

---

CHECKLIST FOR CHOOSING A CLOSE READING TEXT

✓ Will it be challenging for your students?

✓ Will it require re-reading for a complete understanding?

✓ Will it necessitate chunking the text for students to grasp the meaning?

✓ Will it need classroom discussion to ensure that students understand?

✓ Will it merit the time necessary to complete a close reading lesson?

Figure 3.1 Choosing a Text

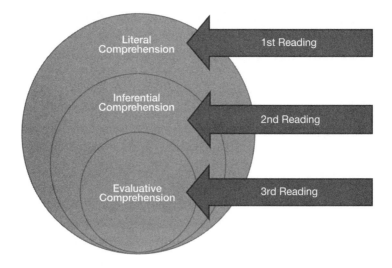

Figure 3.2 Levels of Comprehension

discourse can be a powerful vehicle for students to collaborate and build off each other's learning. Looking at your text, do you believe that they will understand on their own, or do you think that they will need to talk about the passage and hear others' perspectives about it in order to obtain a deeper understanding? Will the process of talking clarify the meaning of the text for them? *Does it merit the time?* This is a crucial question. Depending on the length of the text, its complexity, your instructional goal, and the skills and motivations of your students, a close reading activity may take a class period or may need to be extended over several days. You need to decide if this particular text is worthy of so much time and effort. If it is, then move on to the second step. If it isn't, then complete the reading as you normally would and save your close reading strategies for a text experience from which your students will truly benefit.

Step 2: Determine Purpose for Reading. A common misconception about close reading is that after we identify a complex text, we simply start reading. The reality is that you need to determine what your purpose for the reading is. What do you want your students to take away from this experience? Is it simple comprehension and appreciation of the text? Is it a particular reading objective, e.g., identifying theme, narrative elements, text structure, author's purpose? Is it an appreciation for a particular genre of writing? Is it as an inquiry method to solve a particular problem? Perhaps it is as a means to deepen the academic rigor in your classroom. Your purpose will guide the close reading activity from beginning to end.

Its value cannot be over-emphasized. If you don't have a purpose, then what is the objective for incorporating this reading into your instruction, and of equal significance, where are you taking your students? Use the purpose as a roadmap for planning the entire close reading activity. At the onset, it should inform how you structure the initial reading, allowing you to clarify why your students are reading the passage as well as set for them a mental anchor through which they can get a foothold on the text. It will also carry you throughout the repeated readings, the corresponding tasks and discussions, and facilitation of classroom discussions. In short, your purpose should be woven throughout every aspect of the close reading activity.

Think about how each reading cycle should move your students closer and closer to your purpose. Using this goal as a target for your work during close reading will ensure that each reading cycle furthers your efforts to reach your purpose and lead ultimately to what you hope to achieve with this passage.

Step 3: Choose a Model. In the coming chapters, you will learn a variety of models that meet specific purposes. Choose one that is appropriate to your text and purpose. Later, you may decide to create your own. In any case, don't begin a close reading activity until you have a model in place.

Step 4: Decide How Students Will Access Texts. The next step is to consider how your students will access the text. Will you read it aloud to them? Will you conduct a shared reading? Will they read in small, collaborative groups, in dyads, or individually? You need to make that choice for each of the reading cycles. For primary grades, you may decide to begin with a read aloud, progress to a shared reading, and then transition to a small-group reading. With upper elementary, it may follow this process, or you may decide to begin with a read aloud, move to a paired reading, and then shift to silent reading. Whatever configuration you select, the decision should be based on moving students closer and closer to independent reading and analysis.

Step 5: Complete First Cycle of Reading and Present Question/Task. The first time students read the passage will be their introduction to the material. Depending on the purpose, you will either pose a question eliciting their understanding after an initial reading or give them a task. The task could range from analyzing vocabulary words to creating a graphic organizer demonstrating their understanding to creating a product (e.g., illustration, demonstration, mobile, song). Both questions and tasks must be text dependent, meaning that the reader can only respond by referring explicitly back to text. Keep this in mind as you construct your questions and tasks throughout the close reading activity. Students must delve back into the text—and not rely on their prior knowledge of the topic.

The key to this particular step is to choose a question/task that sets the groundwork for students to develop a sense of the author's words and be able to paraphrase the passage into their own words. By doing so, students will be prepared to discuss their reading after the first cycle and be primed to move to more rigorous thinking during the second cycle.

Step 6: Provide Time for Discussion. This step devoted to discussion is critical for students. It is during this time that they share their thinking, making their thinking "visible" to you. Here is your opportunity to assess what they understand, what misconceptions they might hold, and what additional support you need to build into the subsequent steps. Without this step, they lose their time to reflect and process the material, and you lose the opportunity to gauge their learning.

For struggling students, you may want to build in time for them to do a think-pair-share so that they have a partner to share with before venturing into a whole-group discussion. You may also choose to have small-group discussions before large-group discussions to further provide a scaffold to their sharing.

Step 7: Complete Second Cycle of Reading and Present Question/Task. After completing the first cycle of reading, your goal is to select the question/task that will propel the students forward to coming closer to your instructional goal. Think about the next step to build from their initial reading. This step needs to build a strong link between the initial reading and the final reading. So, choose carefully.

Step 8: Provide Time for Discussion. Again, ensure that you schedule enough time for class discussion. Provide the opportunity for students to talk about what they are learning and to grapple with confusing aspects of the passage. Without this step, students often move through the reading process in a passive stance with little real thinking behind their reading.

Step 9: Complete Third Cycle of Reading and Present Question/Task. The final step must build that last link to your instructional purpose. It has to deepen their thinking, moving from noticing details about the text to grasping the author's big ideas. From here, your students should be able to interpret the passage as well as offer evaluative statements about its content.

One way to construct a well-designed close reading activity is to determine your instructional goal and then work backwards. For example, if you want your students to be able to form an opinion about the author's use of metaphors, you will start at the third reading cycle with asking students to make a judgment about how well the metaphors worked in the passage and if they made the text more interesting for the reader. By the second cycle, however, you will need for them to interpret the metaphors. If they cannot interpret them, they will not be capable of judging their effectiveness. Still thinking in reverse, consider what must come before students can interpret the metaphors—they must be able to identify them. Thus, in the first cycle, students should be given the task of locating the metaphors found in the passage. With that instructional plan in place, the close reading activity would like this:

| Identify metaphors | → | Interpret metaphors | → | Evaluate metaphors |

Using a backward design will foster a clear line of thinking for students and ensure that your close reading lesson plan will be designed intentionally and purposefully to reach your instructional goal.

Step 10: Provide Time for Discussion. Step 10 embodies the final piece of the cognitive framework that close reading builds for readers. By this point, students should be able to use each of the previous steps to speak with confidence about the passage and be prepared to meet your instructional goal. If, however, you feel that students require additional scaffolding and/or additional time to analyze the text, then you may elect to add a fourth reading cycle.

Scaffold the Implementation

Even with a framework in place, you may find presenting complex text to your students a difficult step. To build their confidence, you can transition them through several linked phases that allow them to learn the procedure of close reading without the anxiety typically experienced when readers attempt to read a challenging text. An additional benefit of using this progression is that it allows you to highlight to students that text can take many forms, including visual and auditory, and that referring back to any style of text is helpful and supports learning.

Initiate with video productions. In the absence of written text, show students a video (featuring an appropriate literary production or an informational segment) appropriate to their age level and content goals. Follow the same Close Reading Framework. Determine the purpose, choose a framework model, and then design a series of three (or more if needed) viewing cycles in which students watch a clip from the video and then react to it through content tasks and dialogue. With each additional cycle, emphasize that additional time to re-view and talk about the clip helps the viewer to understand the content.

Move to oral text. Use the framework with a piece of text that is presented orally—through a read aloud or an audiotape. This step takes away the support of visual literacy but retains an auditory component as a base to center student understanding while still withholding the task of students approaching the text independently. Again, follow the Close Reading Framework, and move sequentially through the steps.

Add picture books. Picture books offer a solid transition to written text while still maintaining visual supports. When planning a close reading activity with these texts, start with the pictures themselves. In fact, students should interpret the visual elements as closely as the text itself, conducting a "close viewing" of the visual information contained within the book. Re-read the book with your students, and incorporate visual- and text-dependent questions.

Begin with "easier" text. Up to this point, you have exposed students to challenging text through the sheltered approach of visual and auditory supports. Now, it is time for them to shift to a more active role, but before combatting text that students find difficult, and perhaps overwhelming, bridge the experience with a more accessible passage. The power of this stage is that students are continuing to build their familiarity and confidence with the Close Reading Framework while navigating through a text in which their success is assured.

Integrate hands-on strategies. If your students falter when asked to analyze text at a deeper level other than literal understanding, consider some simple hands-on strategies that will provide an intermediate step. Follow the Close Reading Framework, however, in place of questions or tasks, ask students to mark up the text. For early primary grades, that may take the form of Wikki Stix (Fisher & Frey, 2013). Easily manipulated and capable of adhering to smooth surfaces, you can use Wikki Stix with your students to circle important words, underline main events, etc., on big books, personal books, and other reading materials. In the upper elementary grades, a reading cycle in the framework may be followed by asking students to number the paragraphs and underline the main idea, to use a colored marker to circle key vocabulary words, or to add post-it notes that detail a summary of the text.

These strategies promote engaging student interaction with the text without the expectation of a thorough analysis of the text. While this should only be a transitional stage, when used collectively, adding kinesthetic strategies to a close reading lesson can only support student learning and provide a differentiated approach to making meaning from text.

Annotate. Annotate. Annotate. Before you ask students to delve deeply into text searching for specific questions or tasks, consider giving them the opportunity to share their understanding of a passage in a uniquely individualized manner. How? Simply encourage students to write down their thoughts about the text in the margins.

They may start by describing whatever their reaction is to the passage but then begin to consider why the author wrote the text, what the author wants the reader to take away from it, how the writing style affects the meaning, etc. Asking students to write brief "notes" onto the page also provides a much-needed link between inner thoughts about the text and how they share that with others in a classroom.

Work together in a jigsaw. With your first truly complex text for students to tackle, you may want to give them the added support of working with a group. A jigsaw activity can be a powerful medium for students to rely on as they begin their journey navigating through the demands of a challenging passage.

For this stage, modify the framework to allow students to chunk the tasks demanded of them. For example, complete the first reading as a read aloud and the second independently—both times without asking any questions or tasks of them. On the third cycle, move students to "home" groups where they will read the text together. Afterwards, assign each student one question/task. It may focus on vocabulary, key ideas, author's style, or whatever best fits your purpose for the text. Instruct students to move to their "expert" groups where one member from each of the home groups is now being represented. While they are working with their expert team members, their only responsibility is to respond to their unique question/task. After an appropriate time, students will return from their expert groups back to their home groups where they will share with their classmates what they learned. After small-group discussion, you will bring their conversation to the whole class, consolidating their thoughts into a cohesive analysis of the passage.

Move toward independence with the help of a friend. After students have worked collaboratively in a small-group setting through jigsawing, use the PEER Review next (Figure 3.3). This close reading model allows partners to work together as they analyze text through four reading cycles. It provides that last transitional step before independent reading. With the scaffolds from this chapter in place, your students should be ready to tackle complex text and close reading!

PEER Review

Try this close reading model for two!

Preview – Title, headings, text features, bold words

What do you think the text will discuss? Why do you think that?

Examine – Key ideas

What are the key ideas of this passage?

Evaluate – Author's purpose/Author's style

Why do you think the author wrote this text?

What do you notice about the author's writing style? Provide examples to support your answer.

Respond – Connections to other texts/media

How is this text similar to/different from other media of the same subject? Use specific details to provide textual evidence.

Figure 3.3 PEER Review

Chapter Summary

Students encounter challenging texts on a daily basis. Many of our more vulnerable students become so overwhelmed that they simply don't know where to begin to make meaning. Close reading strategies offer them a solid bridge to bring them together with text in a purposeful context designed to support them throughout the reading process.

The Close Reading Framework provides a structured approach to scaffolding students through analyses of challenging texts with ten steps. Step 1: Identify the text; Step 2: Determine purpose for reading; Step 3: Choose a model; Step 4: Decide how students will access texts; Step 5: Complete first cycle of reading and present question/task; Step 6: Provide time for discussion; Step 7: Complete second cycle of reading and present question/task; Step 8: Provide time for discussion; Step 9: Complete third cycle of reading and present question/task; and, Step 10: Provide time for discussion. Adhering to these steps allows students to progress through a piece of text with increasing understanding and appreciation in a measured, deliberate course.

While some students may be equipped to launch into complex text with ease, others may require intermediate steps to pave the way as they begin to build their confidence with text and their own abilities. For those students, scaffolding the implementation of close reading may itself be necessary. Working through a continuum of support systems with each stage moving students closer and closer to independence, you may find it helpful to initiate students with video productions, move to oral text, try a picture book, begin with "easier" text, integrate hands-on strategies, practice annotating, and finish up with jigsawing and PEER Review.

Book Study

Reflection Questions

Chapter 3: An Overview of Close Reading Strategies

1. What are the ten steps of the Close Reading Framework?

2. How significant is purpose to developing a close reading lesson? Why?

3. Why is a backwards design used to craft a close reading lesson?

4. What are some ways in which you can introduce close reading to your students?

5. How would you determine if a text was "worthy" of the time needed to conduct a close reading lesson?

6. *TASK*: Construct a close reading lesson using the ten steps of the framework.

4

Reading Across Literary and Informational Genres

Every text has its own unique features, ambiguities, and challenges. So, how can you expect to use the same close reading strategy for every poem or passage a student encounters? You can't. Your approach to each text must be tailored not only to that particular piece but also to your instructional purpose for reading it. If not, you are doing a disservice to the text and to your students.

When considering how to interpret a piece, the first consideration must be dependent on the text itself. How a reader analyzes a passage differs widely between literary and informational genres. That becomes doubly important if your purpose in reading the text is to familiarize your students with a particular genre, to conduct a genre study, or to utilize the characteristics of the genre as a means to interpret the meaning. In these cases, each distinctive genre necessitates a correlated framework that highlights how a reader approaches a text representing this type of writing.

In literary works, each framework focuses on how their shared characteristics differ from one genre to the next—what distinguishes them to the reader and how to use these traits as a means to examine the story. For example, while the literature that students encounter will all contain characters, settings, problems, and solutions, how these narrative elements are treated within the texts vary and affect both the plot itself as well as the resulting theme that emerges from its telling. Analyzing these commonalities in a close reading activity, then, allows students to clarify the central qualities of each genre and use them as a lens to understand, analyze, and interpret their works.

To aid you when your purpose is to look at genre characteristics, there is a model for each genre. They suggest the ways in which students will access text, potential questions and discussion guides, and extra scaffolds that offer more hands-on, kinesthetic strategies meant to engage and support student learning. You should, however, make whatever modifications to the frames that are required to meet the needs of your students.

Literary Genres

Literature refers to stories that are invented through the imagination of the mind with different literary genres sharing some similar characteristics, such as adhering to a universal narrative text structure (see Figure 4.1). They all have characters, settings, and major events that encompass a problem and solution. These genres also contain inherent lessons and themes from which the reader should learn. Despite these commonalities, how characters, settings, and events interact with one another is particularly unique to each genre; consequently, the themes that emerge from their stories also reflect different motifs, or recurring ideas.

With that understanding in mind, if your goal is to direct students' thinking toward the purpose of identifying the author's message, or theme, encapsulated within the narrative, then focus their attention on how the narrative elements interact with one another to develop that message. The Close Reading Frameworks found on the following pages are designed to aid you in that work. Each spotlights not just the commonality of narrative elements, but more significantly, how the narratives differ from genre to genre and ultimately guide the reader to determine the author's message for telling the story. As you work with your students, then, emphasize the narrative elements through focused genre studies, close reading activities, and analyses of the similarities and differences among literary genres. These frameworks will help you in that process.

Fantasy. Characters in fantasy stories may live in settings shrouded in the imaginary or supernatural, but they behave in ways that make sense and seem believable. These settings often play a role in the story itself with time and place impacting the plot and character development. Another primary distinction for the fantasy genre is that the problem and solution are tied to these mystical events.

Folklore. Stories classified as folklore are traditional stories passed down through the generations that derive from an oral tradition. Commonly used to explain the world around them or to teach lessons, this genre includes fables, fairy tales, legends, pourquoi stories, tall tales, and trickster tales. They are found in cultures throughout the world and share common characteristics, such as flat characters who tend to be one-dimensional with a single character trait defining them, e.g., kind, brave, selfish. Vaguely described settings such as "once upon a time" or "long, long ago" in a briefly-worded place such as "in a forest" allow the reader to imagine what it might look like. As they were originally told to teach younger generations, these stories tend to contain motifs like "good versus evil" and "right versus wrong."

Historical fiction. Narratives taken from a historical perspective are typically perceived to require student prior knowledge and teacher frontloading of the content. In contrast, a primary attribute of close reading activities is that students should complete a "cold reading" of the material. Using a Close Reading Framework will bridge that gap as students consider how characters in historical fiction behave, what clues the reader can identify in the passages to discover the setting as well as how the problem and solution must be tied in some way to the time period while still holding a universality common to all times, places, and peoples.

Mystery. When students understand that the puzzles in mysteries are the problem of the story and that the solution to the mystery is the same as the solution to the problem, this genre becomes much easier to explore and evaluate. Likewise, the characters and settings in the mysteries are all tied to the puzzle in some way; they function as pieces of the puzzle. Mysteries are the perfect genre for close reading as you need to read analytically and refer back to the text for clues.

Genre	Characters	Setting	Problem	Solution	Common motifs
Fantasy	Characters may have special powers but behave in ways that are plausible; animals may have human characteristics	Imaginary world where magic or the supernatural is common—may be another world; no specific time necessary	Character's problem is tied to this fantasy setting	Solution is also tied to the setting	Good vs. evil; right vs. wrong
Folklore • Fables • Fairy tales • Legends • Pourquoi tales • Tall tales • Trickster tales	One-dimensional flat characters who can usually be defined by a single trait; may be human or animals	Vague setting (e.g., long, long ago) but may reflect the tale's culture (e.g., European castle, African village)	Based on the conflict between virtue and vice (e.g., generosity/ selfishness, caring/ cruelty)	Commonly resolved by the virtuous character being rewarded	Good vs. evil; right vs. wrong
Historical fiction	May be fictionalized, real historical figures, or a combination	Set in a real historical time and place	Stems from the historical setting and reflects the happenings of that setting	Solution is realistic to the time period and location	Motifs related to social and political aspects of the time period

Figure 4.1 Genre Matrix

Genre	Characters	Setting	Problem	Solution	Common motifs
Mystery	Main character commonly investigates the mystery; all other characters tied to the mystery in some way (e.g., victims, suspects, witnesses)	Can be set at any time and any place	Problem revolves around the mystery, or puzzle, to be solved	Resolution of the problem comes from solving the mystery	Good vs. bad; crime doesn't pay
Mythology (Superhero narratives are sometimes referred to as modern myths)	Characters are often not human (e.g., gods and goddesses) but may be mortal or hero-based characters	Place is relevant to the culture from where the myth derived and the time is set in the past	Problem stems from explaining natural phenomena, relationships among the characters (e.g., gods and mortals), or obstacles to overcome (hero quest)	Resolution typically explains how characters react to the problem and how it affects the mortal world	Motif is directly related to the purpose of the myth (e.g., guidelines for moral living, offer a role model as in the hero quests, reward of goodness vs. punishment for evil)
Realistic fiction	Imaginary characters who behave in realistic ways	Set in a real place in contemporary times	Believable problem that must be solved by the character	Resolution of the problem is rationale	Wide range; can be easily applied to reader's life
Science fiction	Characters may be human, alien, robot, or animal	Usually set in the future with elements of fantasy and realism; place will be based in outer space or alternate world	Reflects a human problem but emerges because of science fiction setting and characters	Solution is rationale within this setting and for these characters	Commonly suggests a warning about the future

Figure 4.1 continued

Mythology. An exciting genre, mythology can be baffling to young readers without instructional support. On the other hand, close reading these stories allows students to make meaning at the most literal level and, through re-readings and structured analysis of the narrative elements, to evaluate their original intent and contemporary relevance. Characters play a substantial role in this analysis. Are they gods, heroes, mortals? Each of these archetypes behaves differently and serves a different role in the narrative. The setting also offers a window into how the plot will develop. The problem and solution may, after the first reading, appear to be contextually bound to an ancient tale, however, after repeated readings, purposeful questioning, and classroom discussion, students should discover that they are indeed relevant to the world in which they live today.

Realistic fiction. One of the most common genres, realistic fiction provides readers a wonderful opportunity to focus less on how narrative elements differ among the varied classifications of literature and more on the narrative elements themselves. Using the framework, students can deconstruct a text into its constituent pieces and then use those pieces to construct meaning, interpret the message, and evaluate the author's effectiveness in crafting the narrative.

Science fiction. Sometimes complicated to understand, students benefit greatly from re-reading, and more importantly for this genre, talking about the text with peers and you. With unusual characters, strange settings, and nuanced problems commonly outside of the experience of younger readers, students can become frustrated and disengaged from the reading. You can mediate that anxiety by involving your students in focused re-readings of a key passage and ongoing opportunities to share their thoughts and beliefs about the text with others.

Poetry. The word *poetry* derives from a Greek verb meaning "to create" or "to make." This action serves two purposes. First, the poet makes a text—a work of art. Then, the reader must make meaning from that text. Unfortunately, a disconnect between the two often takes place. While poems are typically brief pieces of text, they can be challenging for students as they struggle to understand poetic structures, to grasp the emotions poets infuse into their words, to determine what message they should take away, and ultimately,

CLOSE READING FRAMEWORK

FANTASY

Step 1: Identify the text.
Choose a story appropriate to your students.

Step 2: Determine purpose for reading.
Characteristics of the fantasy genre

Step 3: Choose a model.
Fantasy

Extra Scaffold:
Sketch the setting, focusing on the details that the author gives to describe the time and place of the story.

Step 4: Decide how students will access texts.
Paired reading/Independent reading/Independent reading

Step 5: Complete first cycle of reading and present question/task.
Question: How do the characters in this story behave? Are they realistic?
What is the setting like for this story?

Step 6: Provide time for discussion.
Emphasize that the setting happens in (contemporary/ future) time in an imaginary place amidst things that could not possibly happen, but the characters behave realistically.

Step 7: Complete second cycle of reading and present question/task.
Question: Describe the plot of the story. What happens in the story?

Step 8: Provide time for discussion.
Talk about the main events with particular attention paid to the problem and the solution of the story.

Step 9: Complete third cycle of reading and present question/task.
Question: What is the lesson/theme of this story? How is it similar to/different from other fantasies we have read?

Step 10: Provide time for discussion.
Discuss how the students arrived at the theme and how it compares to other fantasies read.

CLOSE READING FRAMEWORK

FOLKLORE

Step 1: Identify the text.
Choose a story appropriate to your students.

Step 2: Determine purpose for reading.
Characteristics of the folklore genre

Step 3: Choose a model.
Folklore

Step 4: Decide how students will access texts.
Read aloud/Shared reading/Shared reading

Step 5: Complete first cycle of reading and present question/task.
Question: How would you describe the characters in this story? What clues does the author give you about them? What is the setting?

> **Extra Scaffold:**
> As students answer questions, record their responses on a story map. Use the story map to guide their understanding of the story's lesson or theme.

> **Extra Scaffold:**
> Add one post-it note for each of the following questions.
> What does the character look like, think, feel, say, and do?

Step 6: Provide time for discussion.
Refer to the text for character descriptions and for a depiction as either good or bad (lower elementary) and flat or round (upper elementary). Discuss the setting as it is described in the text.

> **Extra Scaffold:**
> Highlight words that depict setting, such as styles of buildings, transportation, language, and clothing.

Step 7: Complete second cycle of reading and present question/task.
Question: Describe the problem and solution of the story.

Step 8: Provide time for discussion.
Talk about the main events with particular attention paid to the problem and the solution of the story. Tie the character's experiences to the problem and solution.

Step 9: Complete third cycle of reading and present question/task.
Question: What is the lesson/theme of this story? What can we learn from the character's experiences?

Step 10: Provide time for discussion.
Discuss how the students arrived at the theme and how it compares to other folklore read.

CLOSE READING FRAMEWORK

HISTORICAL FICTION

Step 1: Identify the text.
Choose a story appropriate to your students.

Extra Scaffold:
Number the main events of the story.

Step 2: Determine purpose for reading.
Characteristics of the historical fiction genre

Step 3: Choose a model.
Historical fiction

Step 4: Decide how students will access texts.
Small-group reading/Paired reading/Independent reading

Step 5: Complete first cycle of reading and present question/task.
Question: How would you describe the characters in this story? Are they real or made-up? Do they behave realistically? What is the setting (i.e., where and when)?

Step 6: Provide time for discussion.
Highlight the potential combination of real and imagined characters and the realistic way they behave. Search for textual details that offer clues about the setting.

Step 7: Complete second cycle of reading and present question/task.
Question: Describe the plot of the story.

Step 8: Provide time for discussion.
Pay particular attention to the problem and the solution of the story—especially as it relates to how realistic the problem and the solution are to the time period.

Step 9: Complete third cycle of reading and present question/task.
Question: What is the lesson/theme of this story? Does the theme provide insights into the time period? Is the theme important to us today as well?

Step 10: Provide time for discussion.
Discuss how the students arrived at the theme and how it compares to other historical fiction pieces read.

CLOSE READING FRAMEWORK

MYSTERY

Step 1: Identify the text.
Choose a story appropriate to your students.

Step 2: Determine purpose for reading.
Characteristics of the mystery genre

Step 3: Choose a model.
Mystery

Step 4: Decide how students will access texts.
Small-group reading/Paired reading/Paired reading

Extra Scaffold:
Make a mystery web with a line connecting for each character showing his/her role in the puzzle.

Step 5: Complete first cycle of reading and present question/task.
Question: How would you describe the characters in this story? How are they related to the puzzle contained in the story? What is the setting?

Step 6: Provide time for discussion.
Point out that all of the characters in the mystery play some role in the puzzle to be solved, and the setting tends to be realistic.

Step 7: Complete second cycle of reading and present question/task.
Question: Describe the plot of the story.

Step 8: Provide time for discussion.
Look at the story through the lens of solving a puzzle. What is the puzzle, and how does each event draw us closer and closer to its solution?

Step 9: Complete third cycle of reading and present question/task.
Question: What is the lesson/theme of this story? How is it similar to/different from other mysteries we have read?

Step 10: Provide time for discussion.
Discuss how the students arrived at the theme and how it compares to other mysteries read.

CLOSE READING FRAMEWORK

MYTHOLOGY

Step 1: Identify the text.
Choose a story appropriate to your students.

Step 2: Determine purpose for reading.
Characteristics of the mythology genre

Step 3: Choose a model.
Mythology

> Extra Scaffold:
> Write in the margins when you find clues to what the main character is saying, feeling, or how he/she changes by the end of the story.

Step 4: Decide how students will access texts.
Read aloud/Small-group reading/Paired reading

Step 5: Complete first cycle of reading and present question/task.
Question: What kind of characters (god, hero, mortal) does this myth have? How do they affect the story? What is the setting for this story?

Step 6: Provide time for discussion.
Point out the character types and how they influence the story.

Step 7: Complete second cycle of reading and present question/task.
Question: Describe the plot of the story.

Step 8: Provide time for discussion.
Emphasize that the character types in the myth influences both the problem and the solution of the story.

Step 9: Complete third cycle of reading and present question/task.
Question: What do you think the purpose of this myth was? Is the lesson/theme of this story connected to its purpose? How?

> Extra Scaffold:
> Circle the problem in red and the solution in green. The solution points you to the lesson learned.

Step 10: Provide time for discussion.
Discuss how the students arrived at the theme and how it compares to other myths read.

CLOSE READING FRAMEWORK

REALISTIC FICTION

Step 1: Identify the text.
Choose a story appropriate to your students.

Step 2: Determine purpose for reading.
Characteristics of the realistic fiction genre

Step 3: Choose a model.
Realistic fiction

Step 4: Decide how students will access texts.
Paired reading/Independent reading/Independent reading

Step 5: Complete first cycle of reading and present question/task.
Question: How would you describe the characters in this story? What is the setting?

Step 6: Provide time for discussion.
Reinforce textual evidence using indirect characterization (what a character looks like, thinks, feels, says, and does) as a means to describe characters. For setting, look for details about where and when the story happens.

Step 7: Complete second cycle of reading and present question/task.
Question: Describe the plot of the story.

Step 8: Provide time for discussion.
Sequence the main events of the story visually (e.g., story map, flow map, sequence of events chart) with particular emphasis on problem and solution.

Step 9: Complete third cycle of reading and present question/task.
Question: What is the lesson/theme of this story? Could this lesson apply to your own life? How?

Step 10: Provide time for discussion.
Discuss how the students arrived at the theme and how it compares to other realistic fiction stories read.

Extra Scaffold:
Underline the main characters. Circle the words/phrases that describe the character. Code each circle.
L = Looks like
T = Thinks
F = Feels
S = Says
D = Does
Draw an arrow from the circled words/phrases to the character described.

CLOSE READING FRAMEWORK

SCIENCE FICTION

Step 1: Identify the text.
Choose a story appropriate to your students.

Step 2: Determine purpose for reading.
Characteristics of the science fiction genre

> Extra Scaffold:
> Themes in science fiction often stem from a message or warning about the future. Does this story do that?

Step 3: Choose a model.
Science fiction

Step 4: Decide how students will access texts.
Small-group reading/Paired reading/Paired reading

Step 5: Complete first cycle of reading and present question/task.
Question: What are the characters? How do the characters behave? Do they act realistically to the setting? What is the setting? What textual details provide clues for the reader?

Step 6: Provide time for discussion.
Detail how characters, although in a science fiction setting, behave in ways that make sense. Refer back to the text for clues in determining the setting.

Step 7: Complete second cycle of reading and present question/task.
Question: Describe the plot of the story.

Step 8: Provide time for discussion.
Emphasize that the problem and solution are typically related to the science fiction setting but reflect human problems.

Step 9: Complete third cycle of reading and present question/task.
Question: What is the lesson/theme of this story? Does it suggest anything about the future?

Step 10: Provide time for discussion.
Discuss how the students arrived at the theme and how it compares to other science fiction stories read.

to learn what meaning poems have in their lives. One method to structure their approach to this genre is to begin with a structural analysis of the poem, then move to examine its content, and finally to develop an interpretation of its meaning—with all three phases dependent on the text and the details they elicit from it.

This range of cognitive demands produces a distinct need for close reading strategies. As with other styles of writing, the first reading cycle should focus on surface understanding of the text. In the case of poetry, it will help immeasurably to focus on individual words and the author's word choice as well as the structure of the poem itself. Structure is often key to understanding a poem as it relates to the reader not just the selection and placement of words (e.g., a haiku structure of three unrhymed lines of five, seven, and five syllables) but also its general intent (e.g., haiku commonly focuses on some aspect of nature). Punctuation is also a part of the structure as it organizes the words into units of meaning for the reader.

During the second reading cycle, readers should begin to build deeper meaning from surface understanding of the text. It may help students to paraphrase individual stanzas or lines of the poem before attempting to summarize the central meaning of the text as a whole.

The third reading cycle builds from the previous two readings to help the reader identify the central message. If students falter at this stage, it helps to review the prior discussions and link that to the inevitable conclusion of what the true meaning for this piece of text may be.

Informational Genres

Nonfiction texts tend to be more challenging for readers for a number of reasons. First, they often demand a certain level of prior knowledge about the material. Second, the vocabulary tends to be more academic and littered with multisyllabic words, which increases text complexity. Third, in contrast to the sequence of events text structure found in literary genres, the text structures vary among informational genres and so require a greater working knowledge of how their respective

CLOSE READING FRAMEWORK

POETRY: Grades K-2

Step 1: Identify the text.
Choose a poem appropriate to your students.

Step 2: Determine purpose for reading.
Characteristics of poetry

Step 3: Choose a model.
Poetry

Extra Scaffold:
This can be done through teacher modeling, paired work, or independently.

Step 4: Decide how students will access texts.
Shared reading/Shared reading/Shared reading

Step 5: Complete first cycle of reading and present question/task—STRUCTURE.
Task: Circle stanzas and number them chronologically. Underline any words you don't know. Circle words that appeal to your senses (words you can see, hear, touch, taste, and feel).

Step 6: Provide time for discussion.
Focus on vocabulary terms and paraphrasing individual stanzas.

Step 7: Complete second cycle of reading and present question/task—CONTENT.
Question: Summarize the poem in one sentence.

Step 8: Provide time for discussion.
Listen to as many summary sentences as possible, charting the commonalities and facilitating discussion about how students developed their summaries.

Step 9: Complete third cycle of reading and present question/task—INTERPRETATION.
Question: What do you think this poem means? Why?

Step 10: Provide time for discussion.
Require students to use textual evidence to support their answers.

CLOSE READING FRAMEWORK

POETRY: Grades 3-5

Step 1: Identify the text.
Choose a poem appropriate to your students.

Step 2: Determine purpose for reading.
Characteristics of poetry

Step 3: Choose a model.
Poetry

> **Extra Scaffold:**
> Use the words underlined by students as a means to utilize context clues to dig deeper into the vocabulary as well as for their importance in the poem.

Step 4: Decide how students will access texts.
Read aloud/Shared reading/Paired reading

Step 5: Complete first cycle of reading and present question/task—STRUCTURE.
Task: Circle stanzas and number them chronologically. Make a note in the margins beside each stanza telling what you think it is talking about. Underline any words that you think are interesting in the poem.

Step 6: Provide time for discussion.
Focus on vocabulary terms and paraphrasing individual stanzas.

Step 7: Complete second cycle of reading and present question/task—CONTENT.
Question: Summarize the poem in one sentence.

Step 8: Provide time for discussion.
Listen to as many summary sentences as possible, charting the commonalties and facilitating discussion about how students developed their summaries.

Step 9: Complete third cycle of reading and present question/task—INTERPRETATION.
Question: What does this poem mean? What message is the poet trying to communicate?

Step 10: Provide time for discussion.
Require students to use textual evidence to support their answers.

structures influence the delivery of the information. Fourth, the central idea may be ambiguous if the reader does not understand the author's purpose in writing (information versus opinion writing). Fifth, students may not be motivated to read for information about a given topic if they have no interest in it.

That said, nonfiction texts have recently come to the forefront of a national dialogue regarding its impact on student learning, especially in the early grades (Duke, 2000; Flowers & Flowers, 2009; Gill, 2009; National Governors Association Center for Best Practices & Council of Chief State School Officers, 2010; Routman, 2000). This may be traced to a number of research studies. For example, in 2000, Duke determined that first-grade classrooms devoted an average of 3.6 minutes a day on informational text. In a 2012 article focusing on informational text, Yopp and Yopp cited their 2006 study, which revealed that in read-aloud selections in preschool through grade three, teachers in the majority of the time utilized narratives (77 percent) or a mixed selection of genre generally consisting of poetry (14 percent), rarely selecting purely informational texts (8 percent).

Reading researchers point to several key reasons why teachers should be conscientious in their use of nonfiction texts. They foster background knowledge and cross-curricular learning, increase access to academic vocabulary, encourage academic rigor, develop awareness of diverse text structures, support varied experiences and classroom discourse, and prepare students for the academic expectations in the upper grades (Akhondi, Malayeri, & Samad, 2011; Flowers & Flowers, 2009; Yopp & Yopp, 2012). They also have the potential to stir excitement in reading that literature sometimes cannot—especially for boys (Brozo, 2002).

As a means to provide consistency in our discussion, we will use the nonfiction framework for elementary grades developed by Williams (2009). Within this model, nonfiction is delineated into three structural categories: narrative, expository, and hybrid. Narrative nonfiction tends to follow a linear flow of information as the author recounts a fact-based story. Examples of this structure include biographies and memoirs. The intent of expository nonfiction is topic based and aims to inform the reader, such as with informational websites, maps, and photos. The final classification is hybrid text, such as newspapers, magazines, and dual-formatted books as in *The Magic School Bus* series.

As you expose your students to a range of nonfiction texts throughout these three structural classifications, we will highlight some examples. From narrative nonfiction, we will explore autobiography, biography, and memoir. We will look at expository nonfiction through the lens of modern informational websites as well as historical primary source documents like maps and photographs. For hybrid texts, we will take a look at newspapers. Lastly, we will consider how to work with textbooks (including math problems), offering strategies and recommendations to equip your students to access this often complex material.

Autobiography and biography. Detailing a true depiction of a real person's life, "biographies are great beginning bridges to nonfiction because they are typically narrative and sequential" (Bluestein, 2010, p. 597). Taken together, biographies and autobiographies afford readers the opportunity to explore the lives and experiences of those who lived exceptional lives alongside those who lived life common to everyday existence.

Memoir. As a narrative, memoirs are autobiographical in nature, recounting specific memories from a person's life. They tend to focus on particularly important personal experiences that had bearing on the author's life. Consequently, the reader should not only read for the pleasure of the story but also for the life lessons learned by the author.

This genre generally encompasses small pieces of text and tends to be succinctly written as it attempts to reveal a significant experience in the life of the author. This allows the reader to grasp the content easier and be able to identify key narrative elements found in the story.

Informational websites. While in 1994 only 35 percent of classrooms had Internet access (Parsad & Jones, 2005), today that statistic has risen to nearly 100 percent. Despite the prevalence of computers in classrooms, a policy report from the National Center for Education Statistics indicates that only 40 percent of the study's respondents often use computers during instructional times (Gray, Thomas, & Lewis, 2010). These statistics are troubling if we consider the expectations that we currently hold for students to be technologically proficient and well-skilled in online reading.

Often referred to as New Literacies, digital text changes how we define literacy (Burnett, 2013), and how we teach must change along with it. Reading online proves to be a highly sophisticated skill that few students have mastered. Substantially dissimilar from the linear structure characterized in traditional text-based reading, online reading comprehension focuses on a problem-solving model in which students search online for materials appropriate to their purpose and can randomly branch off to new text sites by accessing hypertext at any given point. Doing so requires recursive reading in what Leu et al. (2011) designate as five specific areas: "(a) reading online to identify important questions, (b) reading online to locate information, (c) reading online to critically evaluate information, (d) reading online to synthesize information, (e) and reading online to communicate information" (p. 7).

To accomplish such comprehensive reading skills, students will require explicit instruction in the use of metacognitive strategies for both traditional and online reading texts (Coiro, 2011) with teachers needing "to thoughtfully guide students' learning within information environments that are richer and more complex than traditional print media, presenting richer and more complex learning opportunities for both themselves and their students" (Leu et al., 2004, p. 1599).

Of greater concern, Mangen (2008) asserts that "one main effect of the intangibility of the digital text is that of making us read in a shallower, less focused way" (p. 408). Combatting this trend will be the use of close reading strategies to encourage students to read digital texts recursively and purposefully. How do you begin? Coiro and Fogleman (2011) recommend that teachers should not develop a lesson plan using web-based learning without first putting forth an instructional purpose.

In addition to these general recommendations, "one must know how to navigate nonlinear text, repeatedly evaluate resources, sift through extraneous materials, infer meaning, and use a range of features to compose unified messages" (Karchmer-Klein & Shinas, 2012, p. 289). Again, using close reading strategies will develop these skills the most effectively with ongoing support systems in place.

Students must also be trained to evaluate websites. Harris (2010) developed a useful tool for students to use as they determine if the website they have visited is worthy of reading. Presented as an acronym, CARS asks students to look at a website for credibility, accuracy, reasonableness, and support. First, students make the determination if they deem the website credible based on a number of components including author's credentials, evidence of quality control such as those found on organization's websites, and written text that doesn't reflect grammatical errors. Second, they look for indicators of accuracy such as when the website is clearly dated and makes specific statements rather than broad generalizations. Third, students consider if the website is reasonable by reflecting if the text is fair, objective, consistent, and moderate in its views. Fourth, and last, they analyze the text for its support. Does it have a bibliography? Does it present information corroborated by other sources? Does it reflect external consistency by being similar to the information presented by other websites? Only after the website has passed the CARS test (Figure 4.2), should students continue reading.

Primary sources. Teachers often neglect to utilize primary sources in the elementary classroom. Typically encompassing artifacts such as maps, photographs, poetry, song lyrics, diaries, speeches, and news articles, they serve to connect the past to the present on a personal level provided by those who lived during a particular time period and develop a world awareness with a relevance that cannot be obtained through other text selection types (Morgan & Rasinski, 2012). In investigating these sources, follow a three-step protocol: 1) describe what obvious information you can glean from the source, 2) analyze what this information reveals, and 3) reflect upon what you, as the reader, can learn from this source in connection to the content subject studied. Following are frameworks for the genres we've just explored.

Credibility

Accuracy

Reasonableness

Support

Figure 4.2 CARS Test for Evaluating Websites

CLOSE READING FRAMEWORK

AUTOBIOGRAPHY AND BIOGRAPHY

Step 1: Identify the text.
Choose an autobiography or biography appropriate to your students.

Extra Scaffold:
– Emphasize that autobiographies and biographies read like a story, but they reveal the lives of real people.
– Complete a flow chart highlighting key events in the person's life.

Step 2: Determine purpose for reading.
Understand and appreciate autobiographies and biographies

Step 3: Choose a model.
Autobiography/biography

Step 4: Decide how students will access texts.
Small-group reading/Paired reading/Independent reading

Step 5: Complete first cycle of reading and present question/task.
Question: Identify the who (subject of the text), what (major accomplishments), when (time period person lived), where (place person lived), how (how person achieved accomplishments), and why of this person's life (why the person chose to direct his/her energies to the respective accomplishments).

Step 6: Provide time for discussion.
Ensure that students have a basic knowledge of the person's life.

Extra Scaffold:
Use the flow chart as a visual support

Step 7: Complete second cycle of reading and present question/task.
Question: Locate characteristics about the person from the text that made him/her unique and special.

Step 8: Provide time for discussion.
Chart the characteristics and accomplishments of the person. Link the characteristics to how they helped the person ultimately reach these accomplishments.

Step 9: Complete third cycle of reading and present question/task.
Question: Sum up this person's life in one sentence. How might the person's life had changed if ___ had happened? Use evidence from the text to support your idea.

Step 10: Provide time for discussion.
Discuss how events and how a person responds to these events shape his/her character and ultimately his/her life.

CLOSE READING FRAMEWORK

MEMOIR

Step 1: Identify the text.
Choose a memoir appropriate to your students.

Step 2: Determine purpose for reading.
Understand and appreciate memoirs

Step 3: Choose a model.
Memoir

Step 4: Decide how students will access texts.
Paired reading/Paired reading/Independent reading

> Extra Scaffold:
> Reading Cycles
> 1   2   3
> Event + Feeling = Life
>   Lesson
> Draw student attention to how the author feels about the events in his/her memoir leads him/her to learning a life lesson.

Step 5: Complete first cycle of reading and present question/task.
Question: Identify the setting (time and place) of the memoir as well as the experience described by the author.

Step 6: Provide time for discussion.
Ensure that students understand the importance of setting in memoir and can identify what experience in the person's life the story describes.

Step 7: Complete second cycle of reading and present question/task.
Task: Circle words that show the reader what the author was feeling.

Step 8: Provide time for discussion.
Emphasize that memoirs reflect the feelings the author experienced during the time he/she is describing.

Step 9: Complete third cycle of reading and present question/task.
Question: What did the author learn from the experience described in the memoir? Use details from the text to support your answer.

Step 10: Provide time for discussion.
Discuss what lesson the author learned from the experience described in the memoir.

CLOSE READING FRAMEWORK

INFORMATIONAL WEBSITES

Step 1: Identify the text.
Choose a text that answers a research question.

Step 2: Determine purpose for reading.
Locate, comprehend, and evaluate informational websites

Step 3: Choose a model.
Informational websites

Step 4: Decide how students will access texts.
Paired reading/paired reading/Independent reading

Step 5: Complete first cycle of reading and present question/task.
Question: Does this website answer your question? Does it pass the CARS test?

Step 6: Provide time for discussion.
Work with your students to use the CARS test step-by-step.

> Extra Scaffold:
> Focus student attention on one particular site text at a time.

Step 7: Complete second cycle of reading and present question/task.
Question: What are the text's main ideas?

Step 8: Provide time for discussion.
Help students to determine the main ideas. This will require guiding them in their viewing and analysis of both written and visual text through multiple pathways.

Step 9: Complete third cycle of reading and present question/task.
Question: How does this help you understand your topic better?

> Extra Scaffold:
> Cite specific evidence from the site text that answers the question posed at the beginning of their search.

Step 10: Provide time for discussion.
Ensure that your students understand that the website is only useful if it furthers their understanding of the topic.

CLOSE READING FRAMEWORK

PRIMARY SOURCES—PHOTOGRAPHS

Step 1:   Identify the text.
          What photograph helps you
          understand the subject?

Step 2:   Determine purpose for reading.
          Analyze primary sources

Step 3:   Choose a model.
          Primary sources

Step 4:   Decide how students will access
          texts.
          Paired viewing/Independent
          viewing/Paired viewing

> Extra Scaffold:
> Focus only on surface details during the first reading cycle. Do not allow students to infer until the second reading cycle. This will allow them to devote all of their attention to what they see before making judgments.

Step 5:   Complete first cycle of reading and present
          question/task—DESCRIPTION.
          Question: Look at the photograph. What do you see?
          Who/what is the subject of the photograph? What is in
          the background?

Step 6:   Provide time for discussion.
          Focus on surface details. Chart for the class what they
          notice the first time they see the photograph.

Step 7:   Complete second cycle of reading and present
          question/task—ANALYSIS.
          Question: What time period is represented? What is the
          tone of the photograph? Is it sad, funny, serious? How
          would you describe this photograph?

Step 8:   Provide time for discussion.
          Continue charting student responses. Require responses
          to be accompanied with textual evidence.

Step 9:   Complete third cycle of reading and present
          question/task—REFLECTION.
          Question: Why do you think this photograph was
          taken? What was its purpose? Who was its intended
          audience? Is it similar to/different from other texts
          you have seen?

Step 10: Provide time for discussion.
          Support students to think deeper about purpose and
          composition as they develop their visual literacy skills as
          well as how photographs should provide additional
          information to traditional text.

CLOSE READING FRAMEWORK

INFORMATIONAL TEXT

Step 1: Identify the text.
Choose an information text appropriate to your students.

Step 2: Determine purpose for reading.
Understand informational texts

Step 3: Choose a model.
Informational texts

> Extra Scaffold:
> Chart details from the text as students extract it.
> Who – What – When – Where

Step 4: Decide how students will access texts.
Small-group reading/Paired reading/Independent reading

Step 5: Complete first cycle of reading and present question/task.
Task: Who or what is the subject of this text? Underline the subject in blue. Is there a when in this text? If a time is included, circle in red. Is there a where in this text? If a place is included, draw a triangle around it in green.

Step 6: Provide time for discussion.
Focus on a surface understanding of the text.

Step 7: Complete second cycle of reading and present question/task.
Task: Draw a box around the big ideas in this text. What important things did you learn?

Step 8: Provide time for discussion.
Work with students to determine what is significant in the text. What makes something important for the reader to remember?

Step 9: Complete third cycle of reading and present question/task.
Task: Write one paragraph that summarizes this text. Refer back to your text mark-ups to help you write your summary. Pretend that you are giving your paragraph to someone who has never read this passage. Would they learn everything they needed to know about the text?

Step 10: Provide time for discussion.
Share as many paragraphs as possible. Talk about the commonalities and differences among their paragraphs. Highlight how they determined what to include. What process did you follow?

CLOSE READING FRAMEWORK

MATH PROBLEMS

Step 1:   Identify the text.
Choose a word problem from a mathematics textbook.

Extra Scaffold:
- Sketch the steps of the word problem to be solved.
- Create a table to help solve the problem.

Step 2:   Determine purpose for reading.
Understand word problems

Step 3:   Choose a model.
Math Problems

Step 4:   Decide how students will access texts.
Read aloud/Paired reading/Independent reading

Step 5:   Complete first cycle of reading and present question/task.
Task: Underline the numbers in the word problem.

Step 6:   Provide time for discussion.
Discuss what each number represents in the word problem. Chart these numbers on the board.

Step 7:   Complete second cycle of reading and present question/task.
Task: Circle the mathematical operation described in the problem.

Step 8:   Provide time for discussion.
Ensure that students use the key words to determine the mathematical operation (Example: addition: total; subtraction: minus; multiplication: product; division: out of). Add the operations beside the numbers in order to create an order of operations.

Step 9:   Complete third cycle of reading and present question/task.
Question: What does the problem ask you to do? What do you have to do to solve this problem? Will your chart answer the question?

Step 10: Provide time for discussion.
Read through the word problem with the class again to ensure that the information that they have extracted correctly solves the problem.

Chapter Summary

Every text is unique. Because of the distinct characteristics each text has—especially within literary and information genres—specific Close Reading Frameworks become a necessity to help students investigate the way texts convey information, how different genres serve different purposes, and how pertinent details can be drawn out in order to construct meaning within these varied texts.

Within literary genres, the narrative structure remains the same, which can make reading literature somewhat easier than information text. The narrative elements themselves, however, operate differently within specific genres. More importantly, how they operate greatly influences not only their place in the narrative but also the plot, the theme, and indeed, the very essence of the storytelling experience.

Nonfiction texts, on the other hand, tend to be more challenging for a number of reasons, such as the prior knowledge needed to access the material, specialized content area vocabulary, varied text structures, embedded central ideas that may be ambiguous, and a lack of student motivation to read expository text. In addition to these broad considerations, nonfiction texts come in a much greater variety of forms. Thus, students must learn the attributes of each of these text types and come to understand that they will alter their approach to text depending on the type that it is, such as in how they must read photographs, memoirs, word problems, and informational websites in unique and prescriptive ways.

Reading a variety of literary and informational text enriches the reader's appreciation of the written word as well as content knowledge. The challenge becomes how to aid students in this undertaking. Close Reading Frameworks provide a structured support system as students read in wider arenas and with greater sophistication of content. With these in place, you can work in tandem with your students to increase their literacy experiences, their comfort in varied textual experiences, and ultimately, their independence as readers.

Book Study

Reflection Questions

Chapter 4: Reading Across Literary and Informational Genres

1. Discuss the narrative elements found in literary genres. How do these narrative elements influence the text?

2. What factors make informational genres difficult for students to read?

3. Explain how you can categorize informational genres.

4. Which do you believe is the most challenging text for students to access—fiction or nonfiction? Why?

5. *TASK*: Create a close reading template for a piece of folklore, a map, or a newspaper article.

5

Reading for Specific Comprehension Objectives

One of the most essential elements in developing a close reading lesson is to have a clear instructional purpose. While we have discussed the imperative of identifying the purpose of the lesson prior to developing the close reading activity so it will guide your reading cycles and discussions, that purpose can be strengthened by considering what literacy objective can be met through the use of that particular text. It cannot be enough to conduct a close reading activity with the goal being only to help students to understand a text. While comprehending at the literal level certainly provides a foundational step in accessing complex text, a specific literacy objective tied to the text will instil greater strength to the lesson—guiding your thinking about the cognitive pathways students will take to arrive at a given point as well as making those pathways known to students.

New Criticism from which close reading is aligned suggests that instruction should always center on the text. This pedagogical viewpoint argues that the first consideration must be a quality text; then, the educator reflects upon how to glean information from its content, i.e., what comprehension skill might lend itself to this undertaking. This belief is unique from those who believe that you focus on the comprehension skill first and select a text to highlight that skill. Here, with close reading, we always look first at the text.

For example, you may select a text and discover that it will help students learn the skills they need to summarize. Consequently, this will be a text that will benefit from a close reading emphasizing how a reader summarizes. In this instance, students would circle important words in the first reading cycle. After discussing why the words were important and how they influenced the text, students would move on to the second reading cycle and underline key ideas. Again, after taking advantage of the follow-up discussion, students would be instructed to summarize the text after the third and final reading cycle. Using these cycles, students first focus on individual words, then on phrases and sentences, and finally on synthesizing these "marked" pieces of the text into a cogent summary. In this way, rather than rushing to the lesson's objective with students uncertain what to do, you chunk the process into manageable tasks, which gradually—with support—lead them naturally to a deeper understanding of the objective as well as to an awareness of how they can summarize text independently.

How do you begin? Using any close reading model (e.g., PEER, Bloom's Taxonomy, Webb's DOK Levels), begin with the end in mind. Consider the literacy objective that you want your students to walk away with at the completion of the lesson. Make that goal your final reading cycle. Then, consider how to support students in arriving at this point in a natural, progressive, authentic way. You need—metaphorically—to draw a line from the beginning, literal understanding of what the text conveys and link the cognitive steps needed for students to be able to achieve the literacy objective in a meaningful manner.

Let's try another example. How would you help your students be able to describe a character in depth using specific details from the text? We know that the last reading cycle will be to ask students to make that characterization with textual support, but the bigger, and more important, question is how do you help students to be able to do this? Think about how good readers glean information from a story that gives them a greater understanding of characters. The first thing they probably notice are the actual descriptive words that the author uses about the characters, like referring to them as "scared," "young," or a "bully." These explicit descriptions, known as direct characterization, offer readers insight at a literal comprehension level. They will also be aware of other "clues" to characters, like what they say, how they look, what they feel, what they think, and what others think of them. Moving deeper to an inferential understanding of the text using these indirect characterization techniques strengthens their grasp of characters. Now, apply this understanding of the scaffolding process to build a close reading lesson. At the first reading cycle, ask students to circle all of the words that the author uses to describe a particular character. Discuss the words that students circled and what these words tell them about the character. At the second reading cycle, instruct students to code the text as in Figure 5.1 and add a descriptive word beside the code that illustrates what that phrase or sentence shows them about the character.

By the third cycle, students have strengthened their understanding enough to make that characterization and have the textual support already circled and coded.

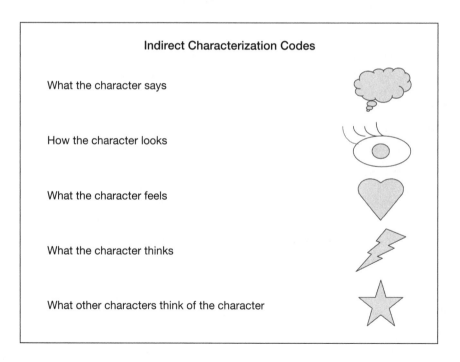

Figure 5.1 Character Codes

Look at the Common Core Anchor Standards in Figure 5.2. The close reading lesson examples in the rest of this chapter provide a scaffolded support system to guide readers into exploring texts more deeply, specifically for the purpose of acquiring active, student-based strategies for developing skills in literacy standards. In other words, while the lessons are teacher-directed, the power of these close reading lessons are in explicitly teaching students the purpose for each reading cycle so that when they are reading independently, they have mastered the steps needed to demonstrate their grasp of the essential literacy skills. We also use similar styles of tasks, e.g., underlining, circling, and coding, so that students are familiar with the process, and focus instead on the objective.

Standard 1—Reading for Details Using Both Literal and Inferential Understanding

Standard 1 from Common Core Standards emphasizes inferential thinking and remains one of the most difficult skills that young readers must learn. With this literacy objective, it will be important to provide explicit directions, model the process that good readers follow when drawing conclusions from the text, scaffold their experiences both in the level of text complexity as well as in the level of inferential thinking, and offer ongoing feedback.

First, begin with explicit directions. Define what it means when readers infer. While a simple explanation is that an inference equates to a guess based on textual evidence, that guess must be based on both the evidence from the text as well as the reader's knowledge. These two components work in tandem to produce a logical inference.

Modeling must come prior to conducting the close reading lesson. Students need to witness how a reader draws conclusions. Begin with a read aloud. After sharing a conclusion that you have drawn from the text, emphasize the process you followed to make such an inference. Using the instructional technique of a think aloud, highlight how you identify explicit information from the text. The next step will prove more problematic and should be described slowly and

COLLEGE AND CAREER READINESS ANCHOR STANDARDS FOR READING

Key Ideas and Details

1. Read closely to determine what the text says explicitly and to make logical references from it; cite specific textual evidence when writing or speaking to support conclusions drawn from the text.

2. Determine central ideas or themes of a text and analyze their development; summarize the key supporting details and ideas.

3. Analyze how and why individuals, events, and ideas develop and interact over the course of a text.

Craft and Structure

4. Interpret words and phrases as they are used in a text, including determining technical, connotative, and figurative meanings, and analyze how specific word choices shape meaning or tone.

5. Analyze the structure of texts, including how specific sentences, paragraphs, and larger portions of the text (e.g., a section, chapter, scene, or stanza) relate to each other and the whole.

6. Assess how point of view or purpose shapes the content and style of a text.

Integration of Knowledge and Ideas

7. Integrate and evaluate content presented in diverse media and formats, including visually and quantitatively, as well as in words.

8. Delineate and evaluate the argument and specific claims in a text, including the validity of the reasoning as well as the relevance and sufficiency of the evidence.

9. Analyze how two or more texts address similar themes or topics in order to build knowledge or to compare the approaches the authors take.

Range of Reading and Level of Text Complexity

10. Read and comprehend complex literary and informational texts independently and proficiently.

Figure 5.2 Common Core Anchor Standards

Source: www.corestandards.org/assets/CCSSI_ELA%20Standards.pdf

clearly, following "The text says . . ." and "I know that . . ." as a vehicle to build a concrete link between how the reader uses the text to form an inference. Chart these categories, drawing lines between multiple examples of the two statements from the text.

Scaffold students' experiences with this literacy objective through initially easy-to-read passages. You want students to focus on the objectives—not be distracted by the need to make literal meaning from the text. As students become more confident and more proficient, slowly increase the level of complexity. Similarly, begin with texts from which readers can easily infer, and gradually increase ambiguity so that it necessitates students to read carefully between the lines to draw conclusions.

Finally, students will require ongoing feedback as the level of rigor escalates. Solicit from them explanations as to what the text said explicitly as well as what text-based guesses they made using their own knowledge, being cognitive of the specific steps of the process by which they infer. Encourage them to be specific and relate their answers back to the text itself.

Standard 2—Theme/Main Idea and Summarization

Elementary readers commonly struggle with recognizing the moral, lesson, or in later grades, the theme, of a fictional narrative. Rather than expect such critical reasoning at the onset, begin with developing literal comprehension and scaffold students toward the goal of inferring from the text using literal understanding as their foundation to build a deeper understanding of the text.

This can easily be done through three reading cycles. In the first cycle, focus on the narrative elements, chunking pieces of text into manageable bits for students to digest. Locate the main character(s), the setting, the problem, and the solution. The next cycle should focus on re-reading for the purpose of summarizing the text. With this grasp of the narrative, use the final reading cycle as a means to identify the lesson of the story. Use the main character as a signpost for what readers can take away from the story. What lesson did the

CLOSE READING FRAMEWORK

ANCHOR STANDARD 1—INFERENTIAL THINKING

Step 1: Identify the text.
Choose a text that lends itself to inferential thinking.

Step 2: Determine purpose for reading.
To learn how to draw conclusions

Step 3: Choose a model.
Inferential thinking

Step 4: Decide how students will access texts.
Read aloud/Shared reading/Paired reading

Step 5: Complete first cycle of reading and present question/task.
Task: Write a brief summary of the text.

Step 6: Provide time for discussion.
Lead a discussion designed to ensure literal comprehension of the text.

Step 7: Complete second cycle of reading and present question/task.
Task: One conclusion that the reader could draw from this text is _____. Look for any direct evidence from the text that would support this conclusion. Underline it, and code it TE (textual evidence).

Step 8: Provide time for discussion.
Review all of the coded passages. Focus on the explicit evidence found in the text that supports the conclusion provided. Emphasize which passages support the conclusion and which do not. Highlight how you made your decision, leading a class discussion to help students determine what passages provide appropriate textual evidence. Chart all correct answers for the class to see.

Step 9: Complete third cycle of reading and present question/task.
Task: Look at the text again. This time search for any passages that don't have specific evidence but do seem to suggest support. Underline these passages, and code them IC (inferential clues).

Step 10: Provide time for discussion.
Review all of the coded passages. Focus on the implicit evidence found in the text that supports the conclusion provided. Emphasize which passages support the conclusion and which do not. Highlight how you made that decision, leading a class discussion to help students determine what passages provide inferential support. Chart all correct answers for the class to see. Then, state the conclusion again, and review that good readers draw conclusions by both looking for specific evidence from the text (explicit details) as well as from what they can guess from the text (implicit details).

main character learn from the story? Encourage students to consider the narrative elements, specifically the problem, to guide their thinking as the problem provides not only the focus of a narrative, but more significantly, it commonly demonstrates what lesson the main character learned because of it. Remind them to look back at their summary as it illustrates the progression of the story. What happened? What was the problem? How was it resolved? What did the character learn from the problem? What did the character learn from the resolution? Finally, what lesson did you, as the reader, take away from this story?

The re-readings will familiarize students with the content of the narrative, instilling confidence in their grasp of the story while giving them multiple opportunities to think about the narrative in a larger framework beyond a simple story. This also allows students to think more critically gradually—rather than after a single reading.

Within nonfiction, determining the main idea requires a grasp of the hierarchical nature of the main-idea text structure. To ensure such an understanding, you need to be explicit in your explanation of text structures, i.e., defining, modeling, and offering guided and independent practice.

For young readers, a "main idea" can be abstract, and they may be perplexed as to how one discerns the focus of a passage. For the struggling reader, the cognitive energy they expend simply to make meaning may fatigue them beyond their abilities to distinguish between details and main ideas. We recommend that you begin by explaining main idea by using the analogy of a house.

All texts have an overarching topic. This topic is usually just a word or two, and in nonfiction text, can be found in a heading or subheading. This topic encompasses everything in that piece of text (e.g., elephants). Beneath the topic comes the main idea(s). Each paragraph will have a main idea (e.g., natural habitats, foods they eat, traveling in herds). The main idea contained in the paragraph must have supporting details to help the reader understand the main idea (e.g., natural habitats—elephants live in Africa; elephants live in Asia; elephants live in India).

Using the house analogy, supporting details are the foundation of a house. Without the foundation, the house collapses. It is the

CLOSE READING FRAMEWORK

ANCHOR STANDARD 2—THEME

Step 1: Identify the text.
Choose a text that lends itself to determining the lesson, moral, or theme.

Step 2: Determine purpose for reading.
To learn how to identify a narrative's theme

Step 3: Choose a model.
Theme

Step 4: Decide how students will access texts.
Shared reading/Small-group reading/Paired reading

Step 5: Complete first cycle of reading and present question/task.
Task: Use crayons, colored pencils, or markers to circle the main character (blue), the setting (yellow), the problem (red), and the solution (green).

Step 6: Provide time for discussion.
Chart student responses, focusing on how each of these elements represent a different part of the story. Emphasize the problem and how the character resolved it (or the character's reaction if someone else solved the problem).

Step 7: Complete second cycle of reading and present question/task.
Task: Write a one-sentence summary of the story.

Step 8: Provide time for discussion.
Encourage students to share their summaries with the expectation that they will include the main character, the problem, and the solution. Again, highlight the problem and how the problem was resolved.

Step 9: Complete third cycle of reading and present question/task.
Question: How does the character react to how the problem was solved? What lesson did the character learn? What lesson did you learn from reading this story? What is the (lesson) theme of this story?

Step 10: Provide time for discussion.
Stress that students should develop the theme from looking at how the character reacts to the resolution of the problem.

foundation (i.e., the details from the text) that come together to allow the main ideas to emerge. These main ideas become the walls of the house, naturally building up from the foundation. These walls, consequently, hold the house up and support the roof, which is the overarching topic of the text.

Each part of the house is crucial. Take away any of the three parts, and the house crumbles. Without the roof, the reader does not understand the purpose of the text, and comprehension may break down. Take away the walls, and there is no information to explain the topic. In the absence of supporting details, the reader lacks sufficient information to understand what the text is attempting to convey. Each part of the "house" has a specific purpose and works together to create a well-written passage (Figure 5.3).

To scaffold their awareness of how text functions to produce meaning, start by focusing on the topic of the passage. Select a close reading that contains a topic heading. Then, devote class discussion to what topic headings tell readers. Make predictions with your students as to what they expect to read based on this topic. Then, draw their attention to the details. Instruct them to mark the phrases or sentences that seem important. Spend time discussing the way in

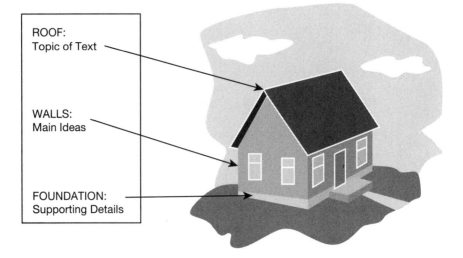

Figure 5.3 Three Crucial Parts of the Text

which details work together to form a main idea. During the last reading cycle, guide them in counting the times a particular detail is mentioned. If it is only once or twice—it is simply a detail. If the same information is mentioned three or more times, it has formed the main idea of the passage.

In concluding the close reading lesson, emphasize that there are three specific steps in determining main idea (Figure 5.4). The topic heading gives readers the first clue (step 1), then the details provide the next set of clues (step 2). Using both helps readers to visualize main idea (step 3) as a level in the hierarchy (or as the construction of a house)—concrete, orderly, and tangible in the reading process.

Summarization tends to be problematic for elementary readers for a number of reasons. First, it requires students to make meaning from an extended text—beyond just sentence-by-sentence comprehension. Second, students must be able to envision the text as one meaningful unit, aware of not just the gist of the passage but also how the sentences work collectively to impart a single intent. Third, they need to be cognizant of what aspects of the text they need to extract in order to make a coherent summary. In effect, students need first to approach the text as one entity, and then, in order to summarize

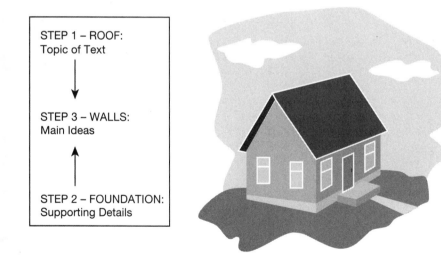

STEP 1 – ROOF:
Topic of Text

STEP 3 – WALLS:
Main Ideas

STEP 2 – FOUNDATION:
Supporting Details

Figure 5.4 Determining the Main Idea

CLOSE READING FRAMEWORK

ANCHOR STANDARD 2—MAIN IDEA

Step 1: Identify the text.
Choose a text that lends itself to determining the main idea.

Step 2: Determine purpose for reading.
To learn how to identify main idea

Step 3: Choose a model.
Main Idea

Step 4: Decide how students will access texts.
Shared reading/Small-group reading/Paired reading

Step 5: Complete first cycle of reading and present question/task.
Task: Circle the topic heading.

Step 6: Provide time for discussion.
Lead a discussion on topic headings and how they prepare the reader for what the text will discuss.
Encourage students to make a text-based prediction about what they expect to read using the topic heading as a guide.

Step 7: Complete second cycle of reading and present question/task.
Task: Underline any phrase or sentence about the topic that seems important.

Step 8: Provide time for discussion.
Talk about the lines that students underlined. What details about the text did they learn? How did the details add to the topic?

Step 9: Complete third cycle of reading and present question/task.
Task: Look at the text again. Each time the same detail (information) is mentioned, number it. If the same detail is mentioned three times, each line should be numbered—1, 2, and 3.

Step 10: Provide time for discussion.
Emphasize that if a detail is listed only once or twice, it is simply an interesting detail. If, however, the same detail is listed more than two times, then it is the main idea. Do a double check. Does the main idea make sense with the topic heading? Does the main idea represent the whole paragraph/passage? If students can answer yes to both questions, they have the main idea!

effectively, view the text again looking for the key pieces that create a cogent summary of the author's words. A final hindrance takes place when students realize that how a reader summarizes differs between fiction and nonfiction text. Fictional text should focus on characters, problems, and solutions—as they are the essential elements of a narrative. Likewise, nonfiction text centers on where (if the text includes a place), when (if the text includes a time), who (or more specifically the subject of the text be it human or not), and what (two or more key details about the subject).

A close reading lesson encourages this course of looking at text. The first reading cycle allows students to gain a cursory understanding of the text. With the second reading cycle, the focus should be digging deeper into the passage and identifying the different pieces of the text that work together—essentially to deconstruct the text. With the final reading cycle, however, the purpose should be to move the reader to reassemble these deconstructed portions of the text to form a clear summary—complete in itself. As these pieces must come together in order for students to create an effective summary, it may be helpful for students not only to identify them within the passage but also to write them on individual index cards so that students can easily see them as individual parts, manipulate them physically to see how they interact with one another when forming a summary, and use them as a support to determine if their summaries accurately reflect the intent of the text.

Standard 3—Narrative Elements

Narrative elements constitute the foundation of elementary comprehension instruction. Without a firm understanding of the inherent structure of a narrative with all of its interlocking pieces, students cannot move forward in examining text at a more critical level. Consequently, the study of narrative elements must be explicit, recurrent, and developed in such a way that students come to identify these component pieces naturally and effortlessly.

While even primary readers can commonly determine characters and settings, students often grapple with the central problem that the

CLOSE READING FRAMEWORK

ANCHOR STANDARD 2—SUMMARIZING (FICTION)

Step 1: Identify the text.
Choose a fictional text with clearly defined narrative elements.

Step 2: Determine purpose for reading.
To learn how to summarize fictional text

Step 3: Choose a model.
Summarizing (Fiction)

Step 4: Decide how students will access texts.
Read aloud/Shared reading/Paired reading

Step 5: Complete first cycle of reading and present question/task.
Task: Circle the main character and the setting.

Step 6: Provide time for discussion.
After discussing with students who the main character is and the setting for the story, instruct them to write the main character's name on one index card and the setting on another. Explain that they have two parts of the story. After re-reading, they will have additional pieces.

Step 7: Complete second cycle of reading and present question/task.
Task: Underline the problem and the solution. Draw an arrow from the problem to the solution.

Step 8: Provide time for discussion.
If students struggle to identify the problem, pose this question. What did the main character want? Link the problem to the solution in explicit terms. What is the solution of the problem? Did the character get what he/she wanted? How? How did the problem end? After the class has established the problem and solution, tell them to use their index cards to create a problem card and a solution card.

Step 9: Complete third cycle of reading and present question/task.
Task: Look back at the four cards while re-reading the text. Do these cards reflect what happened in the story?

Step 10: Provide time for discussion.
Encourage students to draft a summary using only their cards. Emphasize that the four pieces together should tell the important parts of the story.

CLOSE READING FRAMEWORK

ANCHOR STANDARD 2—SUMMARIZING (NONFICTION)

Step 1: Identify the text.
Choose a nonfiction text.

Step 2: Determine purpose for reading.
To learn how to summarize nonfiction text

Step 3: Choose a model.
Summarizing (Nonfiction)

Step 4: Decide how students will access texts.
Shared reading/Small-group reading/Paired reading

Step 5: Complete first cycle of reading and present question/task.
Task: Does the text happen in a certain place. If it does, circle it. If it doesn't, as in some texts, simply keep reading. Does the text happen at a certain time? If it does, draw a box around it. If it doesn't, as in some texts, keep reading.

Step 6: Provide time for discussion.
These first two elements tend to be the easiest to locate. Some texts, however, do not contain them. Students should be aware that science texts often do not include a where or when. If the text does possess these elements, instruct students to write the where on one index card and the when on another index card.

Step 7: Complete second cycle of reading and present question/task.
Task: What is the who (subject) of the text? Underline it. What are at least two important facts (details) you learned about the subject. Underline them, and number them.

Step 8: Provide time for discussion.
After establishing with the class the subject of the text and important details about it, encourage them to create an index card for the subject as well as one for the key details.

Step 9: Complete third cycle of reading and present question/task.
Task: Look back at the four cards while re-reading the text. Do these cards reflect important information from the text?

Step 10: Provide time for discussion.
Encourage students to draft a summary using only their cards. Emphasize that the four pieces together should tell the important parts of the text.

main character faces and the story's resolution. Sometimes, they become embroiled within the narrative and identify relatively minor problems within the sequence of events as critical to the story. Similarly, they struggle with the solution, failing to link these two components together. Readers cannot determine the solution without first working backwards to locate the problem. They do not function separately; rather, they exist as two halves of one whole.

In a close reading lesson, a simple scaffolding strategy is to chunk the text and the tasks we expect of students. Begin by asking students to pinpoint the main character and the setting. Using that information as a means to ground their understanding of the narrative as a whole, instruct them to search for the main problem that the main character has and how he/she solves that problem. Finally, bind these elements together with a sequence of events. Students should be able to demonstrate what happens with the character at the beginning of the narrative, when the problem surfaces, the way the problem is resolved, and how the character responds to that resolution. For younger readers, this sequence may only entail a beginning, middle, and ending. For older students, the events should be expanded to provide further detail about the narrative. An additional scaffold for struggling readers would be a visual support in which students create a timeline of events and then insert where the main character, problem, and solution occur within that sequence.

Standard 4—Vocabulary

Vocabulary is akin to the bridge to comprehension. Unfortunately, it also remains the key stumbling block to struggling readers. Without a warehouse of vocabulary knowledge at their disposal, comprehension falters as students devote all of their cognitive energy to reading word by word, thus losing the meaning of the text as a whole.

Various vocabulary development strategies exist that can be used instructionally. You may elect to provide a grade-level appropriate vocabulary list for your students. Another option is to focus instruction on morphology (i.e., root words, prefixes, and suffixes). You may also choose to teach vocabulary implicitly through the natural course

CLOSE READING FRAMEWORK

ANCHOR STANDARD 3—NARRATIVE ELEMENTS

Step 1: Identify the text.
Choose a fictional text with clearly defined narrative elements.

Step 2: Determine purpose for reading.
To learn how to identify narrative elements

Step 3: Choose a model.
Narrative Elements

Step 4: Decide how students will access texts.
Read aloud/Paired reading/Independent reading

Step 5: Complete first cycle of reading and present question/task.
Task: Circle the main character, and draw a box around the setting.

Step 6: Provide time for discussion.
Discuss with students who the main character is, emphasizing how they identified the main character, as well as the setting of the story.

Step 7: Complete second cycle of reading and present question/task.
Task: Underline the problem and the solution. Draw an arrow from the problem to the solution.

Step 8: Provide time for discussion.
Draw student attention from the problem back to the main character. What did the main character want? What the character hopes to attain and struggles with is the problem. Looking specifically at that problem, ask students to explain how that problem was solved in the story. Did the character get what he/she wanted? How? What happened?

Step 9: Complete third cycle of reading and present question/task.
Task: Place a number by each main event (i.e., 1 by the beginning, 2 by the middle event, and 3 by the end of the story).

Step 10: Provide time for discussion.
Center the discussion on how each of the narrative elements are critical to the story. Take one away, and the story collapses. Each functions as part of a greater whole.

Extra Scaffold:
Create a timeline of the sequence of events. Draw an arrow between the events showing the direction of the action.

Additional Scaffold:
Using the timeline, place the words "main character" above the event when he/she is introduced, the word "problem" when the reader first discovers what the character wants, and "solution" when the problem is solved. (If the timeline is accurate, those events should already be highlighted. This extra step of physically adding the narrative elements serves only to strengthen students' conception of these elements within the text itself.)

of reading, focusing on contextual analysis to determine unknown meanings. Implicit vocabulary can be a powerful instructional practice for students. It is in this context that students see vocabulary terms in authentic contexts and can practice their skills in determining the meaning of unfamiliar words.

With the strength of developing vocabulary through contextual analysis, a close reading lesson for vocabulary in this chapter will emphasize context clue skills. Through the repeated readings, deeper analysis, and a structured scaffold, close reading provides a natural framework for supporting students.

Standard 5—Text Structure

Text structure requires an awareness of how text functions as a single entity as well as how its component parts operate together to create one meaning. For students to utilize this understanding in their reading, they must also appreciate that each of these components serves a purpose. Take one away, and the text collapses.

For young readers, we begin that foundational understanding with the concept of beginning, middle, and end. Students must not only be able to identify those segments of the text but also more importantly recognize how one builds from the other to create a coherent narrative. The first step in this understanding is for students to be capable of locating these pieces within a story.

Close reading will allow students multiple readings so that they become more familiar and comfortable with the story as they transition to how these individual pieces fit together. First, ask students to locate the beginning of the story. Spend time discussing what happens at the beginning. For example, the reader learns of characters and the setting. Next, encourage students to look at the story again, searching for the middle of the story. While the middle of the story will be physically somewhere in the center of the narrative, remind students that by the middle, you are expecting them to think about the problem that the character faces and what is taking place within the story about the problem. This is where they will find the action of the narrative. During this stage of the discussion, ensure that

CLOSE READING FRAMEWORK

ANCHOR STANDARD 4—VOCABULARY

Step 1:   Identify the text.
Choose a text with some unfamiliar words. Be certain that word complexity is not so difficult as to make context clues impractical.

Step 2:   Determine purpose for reading.
To learn how to use context clues to determine unknown word meanings

Step 3:   Choose a model.
Vocabulary

Step 4:   Decide how students will access texts.
Shared reading/Small-group reading/Independent reading

Step 5:   Complete first cycle of reading and present question/task.
Task: Circle any unfamiliar words.

Step 6:   Provide time for discussion.
Discuss with students which words they didn't recognize. Post those words where they can be seen by everyone in the class. After assigning small groups one vocabulary term each, explain that the class will practice four ways to understand unfamiliar words. First, they will look carefully to see if the author may have given a definition. Second, they will re-read the sentences around the vocabulary term to see if they can get a general idea of what the word may mean.

Step 7:   Complete second cycle of reading and present question/task.
Task: Re-read the passage. Look carefully. Does the author define the word for you? Can you understand the term from re-reading the sentences around it? Did you get the gist of the word?

Step 8:   Provide time for discussion.
Go through each small group's assigned word. Encourage them to explain to the class how they used the context clues to help them understand the word. If one of these contextual analysis methods worked, mark through that word for everyone to see. Assign that small group another word that could not be determined from the first two methods. If a word has yet to be understood, continue on

to the third reading cycle and the final two contextual analysis methods.

Step 9: Complete third cycle of reading and present question/task. Task: Look at the word again. Do you see any words that are similar or synonyms? Finally, look to see if there are any words surrounding your vocabulary term that are opposite or antonyms.

Step 10: Provide time for discussion.
Continue with the same discussion as in Step 8.
Emphasize the four context clue methods: definition, gist, synonym or restatement, and antonym. By the end of this lesson, all of the words should be defined.

students find the central problem and can describe what action is taking place. Finally, ask students to look at the text one more time to decide what the ending is. Emphasize that the ending should tell the reader how the character's problem was solved. It may physically be near the end of the narrative, but the students' task is to locate the problem's resolution. The discussion with students should highlight this last step—but also review the narrative as a whole, moving from beginning to middle to end.

Nonfiction arranges text in specific ways based on the most effective way to convey information. Common text structures include chronology, cause and effect, comparison, and problem and solution. Each of these serves a specialized purpose. Chronology acts as a vehicle to sequence key events. Cause and effect suggest an event with preceding causes leading up to this effect. Comparison serves as a means to illustrate similarities and differences among two or more subjects. Problem and solution reveals problems and the resulting solution to these issues. The information, then, is formatted by the author to benefit from whichever text structure best explains the content.

CLOSE READING FRAMEWORK

ANCHOR STANDARD 5—TEXT STRUCTURE (FICTION)

Step 1: Identify the text.
Choose a text with a clearly defined beginning, middle, and end.

Step 2: Determine purpose for reading.
To learn how to analyze text structure

Step 3: Choose a model.
Text Structure

Step 4: Decide how students will access texts.
Read aloud/Paired reading/Independent reading

Step 5: Complete first cycle of reading and present question/task.
Task: Look for the characters and setting. Then, draw a circle around the beginning of the story.

Step 6: Provide time for discussion.
Emphasize what happens in the beginning of a story.
Remind students that the beginning introduces the story.

Step 7: Complete second cycle of reading and present question/task.
Task: Look this time for the main character's problem. What actions are taking place? This should be the middle of the story. Draw a box around this part of the story.

Step 8: Provide time for discussion.
Focus on the action of the middle of a narrative. Ensure that students found the central problem.

Step 9: Complete third cycle of reading and present question/task.
Task: Look for the solution to the main character's problem. How is it solved? What happens? Draw a triangle around the ending of the story.

Step 10: Provide time for discussion.
Stress to students that the ending of a story is the end of the action and shows the reader how the problem is solved.

The reader can use his/her knowledge about text structure in two important ways. First, recognizing the text structure will afford a style of frontloading whereby the reader recognizes the structure and can then anticipate the way in which the information will be presented. For instance, a chronological text structure would indicate to the reader that the text follows a specific sequence, thus, the reader needs to search the text for these individual events in order to understand the text better. Second, the text structure itself acts as a means to organize the information in a meaningful way. For example, if the reader recognizes the text structure as compare and contrast, the next step is to search for ways in which the subjects of the text are similar and ways in which they are different, in effect creating cognitive placeholders for content. Thus, it influences the way the reader approaches the text as well as how the reader begins to catalog and store the information.

How does the reader investigate text structure? A simple way is to familiarize your students with signal words for each of the structures. These signal words function as guideposts directing students to the correct text structure, and by extension, to how to approach the text (see Figure 5.5).

Standard 6—Point of View

Point of view requires students to move beyond literal comprehension and consider text through the lens of inferential understanding and critical analysis. To do this, students must first grasp the text's meaning at a surface level. Then, moving further into the under-currents of the text's intent, they need to reflect on who is narrating this story and why the narrator selected by the author has significant impact on the telling of the narrative. Finally, they should consider how the telling of this narrative could be altered based solely on whose point of view the reader sees. Cue words are shown in Figure 5.6.

These are not simple expectations. For the struggling reader, the first step of literal comprehension may in itself be a stumbling block. Through a close reading lesson, however, you can support students

CLOSE READING FRAMEWORK

ANCHOR STANDARD 5—TEXT STRUCTURE (NONFICTION)

Step 1:   Identify the text.
Choose a text with a clearly illustrated text structure.

Step 2:   Determine purpose for reading.
To learn how to identify specific text structures

Step 3:   Choose a model.
Text Structure

Step 4:   Decide how students will access texts.
Shared reading/Shared reading/Small-group reading

Step 5:   Complete first cycle of reading and present question/task.
Task: Highlight the signal words in this text. What text structure is this?

Step 6:   Provide time for discussion.
Review the signal words from the text. Reinforce with students what these signal words tell the reader about the text.

Step 7:   Complete second cycle of reading and present question/task.
Task: Use the information organizers to record key details from the text.

Step 8:   Provide time for discussion.
Ensure that students have included all of the pertinent information they should have gleaned from the text. Emphasize how the information organizers help them to understand the text and to store the important information in meaningful ways.

Step 9:   Complete third cycle of reading and present question/task.
Task: Looking back at the signal words highlighted and the information organizers completed, re-read the text and then write a one-paragraph summary.

Step 10: Provide time for discussion.
Listen to as many summaries as possible. Stress how understanding the text structure helps good readers approach text and understand it more effectively.

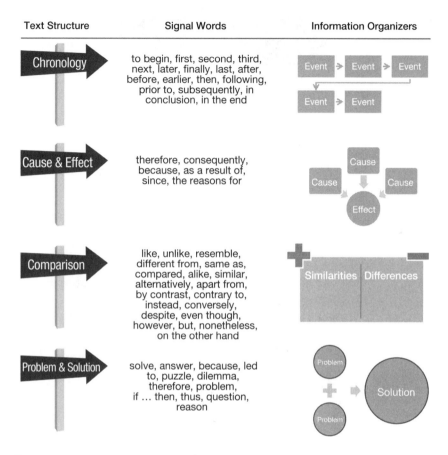

Text Structure	Signal Words	Information Organizers

Chronology — to begin, first, second, third, next, later, finally, last, after, before, earlier, then, following, prior to, subsequently, in conclusion, in the end

Cause & Effect — therefore, consequently, because, as a result of, since, the reasons for

Comparison — like, unlike, resemble, different from, same as, compared, alike, similar, alternatively, apart from, by contrast, contrary to, instead, conversely, despite, even though, however, but, nonetheless, on the other hand

Problem & Solution — solve, answer, because, led to, puzzle, dilemma, therefore, problem, if … then, thus, question, reason

Figure 5.5 Text Structure Guideposts

First-Person Narration

I, me, we

Third-Person Narration

he, she, they, them

Figure 5.6 Point of View Cue Words

CLOSE READING FRAMEWORK

ANCHOR STANDARD 6—POINT OF VIEW

Step 1: Identify the text.
Choose a text with a clearly observable point of view.

Step 2: Determine purpose for reading.
To learn how to identify point of view and analyze its implications on narratives

Step 3: Choose a model.
Point of View

Step 4: Decide how students will access texts.
Read aloud/Small-group reading/Small-group reading

Step 5: Complete first cycle of reading and present question/task.
Task: Circle the words listed from the Point of View Cue Words chart.

Step 6: Provide time for discussion.
Discuss which words students selected. Draw the connection between the pronouns and who is telling the story. Establish with the students whether the narrative is first person or third person.

Step 7: Complete second cycle of reading and present question/task.
Question: Look back at the telling of the story. What does the narrator tell the reader? Would the story change if a different character told the story? Why?

Step 8: Provide time for discussion.
Differentiate among the points of view as well as how students think the story may change if a different character told the story. Assign small groups of students different characters.

Step 9: Complete third cycle of reading and present question/task.
Task: Look at the story again. Now, retell the ending of the story from a different character's point of view.

Step 10: Provide time for discussion.
Allow time for each small group to retell the ending of the narrative from their character's point of view. Emphasize how differently the story is related based on who tells it.

in their examination of narratives and guide their understanding of the inherent importance of point of view and how point of view shapes the stories they read.

Standard 7—Diverse Text Formats and Media

Diverse media can be challenging for students as classrooms in the past have used traditional texts from trade books, anthologies, etc. Today's classrooms expect students to be equally comfortable with analyzing visual texts (e.g., pictures, graphs, charts,), audio texts (e.g., taped interviews), multimedia (e.g., video productions), and digital texts (e.g., online reading resources). This escalation of how we define texts has transformed the educational landscape.

Before we transition students to this range of diverse media, we can begin with the simplest version of what it means to look beyond traditional written text—the inclusion of illustrations and photographs. These are the most familiar to students. They abound in all texts, whether traditional or digital. Lastly, they offer a concrete link with written text that allows students to begin thinking about different ways we access information in a secure, non-threatening context.

With close reading, students have the opportunity to see how written text and visual images connect to create a seamless, coherent understanding of the text. In short, they function in tandem to illuminate the author's meaning. To demonstrate this relationship to students, first draw their attention only to the visual images of the text, encouraging them to gather as much information as possible—whether from a fiction or nonfiction text. Then, add the text. How does this new information strengthen what they learned visually? The final step of the process should induce students to consider what can be learned visually as well as what can be discovered from the written word. What information is repeated through both information versions? Is one better? Does one version of information provide more detail? How? Through a thorough analysis and discussion of this topic, students begin to value the strengths of different media and alter how they approach these media in unique ways.

CLOSE READING FRAMEWORK

ANCHOR STANDARD 7—DIVERSE TEXT FORMATS AND MEDIA

Step 1:   Identify the text.
Choose a text that includes illustrations or photographs.

Step 2:   Determine purpose for reading.
To learn how to pull information from both written text and visual imagery

Step 3:   Choose a model.
Diverse Text Formats and Media

Step 4:   Decide how students will access texts.
Shared reading/Guided reading/Independent reading

Step 5:   Complete first cycle of reading and present question/task.
Task: Look at the illustrations/photographs in this text. What can you see? What is happening? What can we learn?

Step 6:   Provide time for discussion.
As students look at the visual images for details about the text, remind them that they are included to enhance their understanding. Each image has a purpose and supports the written text in some way. Chart their findings under the heading of Illustrations/Photographs.

Step 7:   Complete second cycle of reading and present question/task.
Task: Look at the written text. What is it about? What are you learning?

Step 8:   Provide time for discussion.
Chart their findings under the heading of Text. Then, ask them to look for similarities in the information they learned from the chart. Draw a line between details included in both columns.

Step 9:   Complete third cycle of reading and present question/task.
Task: Look at the story again. Now, look for the details only listed in one column. Can you find that detail repeated in both places—the written text and the illustrations/photographs?

CLOSE READING FRAMEWORK

Step 10: Provide time for discussion.
Add those details that students located and draw a line between the two columns. For those that they could not locate, lead a discussion as to what that tells us as readers. Could the information only be shared through written text or visually? Do you think the author chose not to include the detail in both places? Is one better than the other for sharing particular types of information?

Standard 8—Evaluate Arguments in Text

Evaluating arguments necessitates a much deeper awareness of not only the text's intent but also the quality of the author's argument, specifically considering the effectiveness of the corresponding reasons and corroborating evidence. This proves challenging as most readers —even those at the secondary level—tend passively to accept the arguments posed by authors. Looking critically at an argument and assessing its relative strength remains a foreign concept for students.

Close reading provides a framework for students to delve into nonfiction text and be critical readers. The first step—as with all tasks requiring critical reflection—is to understand the text's meaning at the literal level. Only when the students have that basic comprehension can they extend their thinking to a more critical lens. At that point, then, students should be equipped to locate the reasons that the author has supplied to support the text's argument. Even reasons are not sufficient to appraise an argument as effective. Once the reasons have been identified, students should move to identifying the evidence. Each of these elements of the argument must be present and must be adequate to make an effective argument. Close reading provides the structure for such thinking, but it will be the ensuing discussion that will alter the way students view argumentative text and their understanding of them.

CLOSE READING FRAMEWORK

ANCHOR STANDARD 8—EVALUATE ARGUMENTS IN TEXT

Step 1:   Identify the text.
          Choose a text which demonstrates an author's argument about a given topic.

Step 2:   Determine purpose for reading.
          To learn how to evaluate arguments

Step 3:   Choose a model.
          Evaluating Arguments

Step 4:   Decide how students will access texts.
          Shared reading/Shared reading/Shared reading

Step 5:   Complete first cycle of reading and present question/task.
          Task: Circle the author's argument.

Step 6:   Provide time for discussion.
          Discuss what argument the author is making. Emphasize to students that they are to separate their own opinions/beliefs about the topic from their objective analysis of how well the author makes his argument.

Step 7:   Complete second cycle of reading and present question/task.
          Task: Underline the reasons that the author gives to support his argument.

Step 8:   Provide time for discussion.
          Lead a discussion about how effective the reasons are that the author provides to support his argument. Again, emphasize that the students must think objectively.

Step 9:   Complete third cycle of reading and present question/task.
          Task: Number each piece of evidence that supports the author's reasons.

Step 10: Provide time for discussion.
          Focus on the quality of the evidence. Is it reliable? Can it be corroborated? Is it sufficient to adequately support the author's reasons? If not, guide a discussion centering what the author could change to make the argument stronger.

CLOSE READING FRAMEWORK

ANCHOR STANDARD 9—MULTIPLE TEXTS

Step 1: Identify the text.
Choose two brief texts about the same topic.

Step 2: Determine purpose for reading.
To learn how to compare and contrast multiple texts about the same topic

Step 3: Choose a model.
Multiple Texts

Step 4: Decide how students will access texts.
Shared reading/Small-group reading/Paired reading

Step 5: Complete first cycle of reading and present question/task.
Question: What are the main ideas of the first text?

Step 6: Provide time for discussion.
Chart the main ideas identified by the students from the first text.

Step 7: Complete second cycle of reading and present question/task.
Question: What are the main ideas of the second text?

Step 8: Provide time for discussion.
Chart the main ideas identified by the students from the second text.

Step 9: Complete third cycle of reading and present question/task.
Question: Is there information listed for only one text found in the other text as well?

Step 10: Provide time for discussion.
Mark the chart so that students can visualize the overlapping information contained in both texts. Then, focus on what is found in only one text. Encourage students to reflect on why a particular text did or did not include information from the other text. Is that significant? Also, reflect on what commonalities the texts share as well as what characteristics create a unique approach to the topic.

Standard 9—Comparing and Contrasting Multiple Texts

Students usually focus on a single text. This expectation has changed in recent times with students encountering multiple texts about the same topic. With the vast quantity of information multiplying daily in the world around them, the necessity for reading beyond one text at a time becomes imperative. What's more, the need to consider more than one viewpoint has only intensified.

In the lower elementary grades, students may only read two common texts. Upper grade students should be exposed to three common texts. This expectation demands that students have guided, structured experiences with more than one text, and it requires classroom instruction to change to meet these needs.

Close reading fosters a change in your instructional planning. It also has the potential to advance student cognition in a gradual, supportive environment. Begin by selecting two very brief texts (perhaps a paragraph each). After students have read both texts, chart the main ideas from the first text. Then, re-read both texts, focusing this time more heavily on the second text. Chart the main ideas from this text as well. Conduct another re-reading, searching for any missing information to include on the charts. Finish the lesson by marking the chart to highlight the similarities and differences between the texts. Emphasize commonalities between the texts' approaches as well as what characteristics make each text unique in its style and approach to the topic.

Chapter Summary

A Close Reading Framework offers a powerful technique for providing explicit instruction on comprehension standards. To garner the full potential, the teacher should emphasize how in each reading cycle the reader's thinking moves closer and closer to understanding the comprehension objective. As such, students should be cognizant of why they are re-reading and what purpose it serves in their understanding of the text.

To plan a close reading lesson on comprehension objectives—as for other instructional purposes—the teacher must work backwards. What is the purpose of the lesson? What must students be able to understand or do to reach that purpose? Each reading cycle should build from the previous one to advance students naturally through the text and their understanding of it.

The tasks themselves should be fairly similar to one another. Circle. Underline. Code. The goal is to create a sense of the familiar so that the only aspect of the lesson that students focus upon is the comprehension objective itself.

In the next chapter, we will consider how to use close reading to deepen academic rigor. Looking at Bloom's Cognitive Taxonomy and Webb's Depth of Knowledge Levels, you will learn how to strengthen student cognition gradually within the context of a single text. You will also find a menu of choices from which to select for students to annotate and respond to text as they re-read. Taken together, we will demonstrate how to leverage one text into multiple expansions of student cognition, encouraging them to think deeper and more reflectively than ever before.

Book Study

Reflection Questions

Chapter 5: Reading for Specific Comprehensive Objectives

1. Close reading stems from the work of New Criticism, which suggests that effective instruction comes not in teaching specific comprehension objectives—but rather from focusing on text. Thus, educators would focus on specific objectives only when they present themselves naturally in quality texts. Do you agree with this philosophy? Do you believe that comprehension work should come from authentic text, or do you believe that students require targeted comprehension lessons where the text is secondary to the skill? Why?

2. Why is purpose important in planning a close reading lesson?

3. What commonalities do you see in the close reading models for specific comprehension objectives?

4. Why is it important to use similar tasks when initially beginning close reading lessons? When do you believe you could begin to transition to different task assignments during the close reading lesson?

5. *TASK*: Design a close reading lesson for a particular comprehension objective with which your students are currently struggling.

6 Reading with Increasing Levels of Rigor

Close reading proves to be an effective instructional tool for helping students to access complex text. More than that, however, it possesses the potential to increase the level of rigor in classrooms. Think back to Chapter 2 and its discussion of the history of close reading. Its origin centers in religious texts as readers were expected to read and re-read, searching for a greater truth than the words on the page. This concept holds true today as students use purposeful re-readings of short pieces of text to probe deeper into a text's meaning and critically analyze its content.

There are several means by which we can construct close reading lessons specifically to function as a means not only to increase reading comprehension of difficult text but also to strengthen student cognition when interacting with texts. First, Bloom's Taxonomy offers critical thinking levels through which students can advance as they continue to examine text. Second, Webb's Depth of Knowledge (DOK) Levels focus cognition on the level of complexity of the task and student outcomes. Third, it is also incumbent on us to provide differentiated, prescriptive instruction for students with the understanding that support will look different for individual children. Thus, we also want to offer a differentiated approach to increasing rigor through the use of choices so that students may read and be responsible for the same text, but the instructional support system in place will change based on individual need. Let's take a look at each of three avenues in which close reading can raise cognitive and instructional rigor.

Bloom's Taxonomy

In 1956, Dr. Benjamin Bloom led a committee of educational psychologists in creating a taxonomy of educational objectives (Figures 6.1 and 6.2). The taxonomy consisted of three main classification systems: affective, cognitive, and psychomotor. Its aim was to aid communication among test examiners and to examine the relationship between education and testing. In the book focusing on the cognitive domain, the committee suggested that "this taxonomy is designed to be a classification of the student behaviors which represent the intended outcomes of the educational process" (Bloom, 1956, p. 12). In effect, then, his work centers on the products that students complete as a means to deepen their cognition. Using this classification system, Bloom found that 95 percent of assessment items encountered by college students required only the lowest level of thinking—at the Knowledge Level—with simple recall of information.

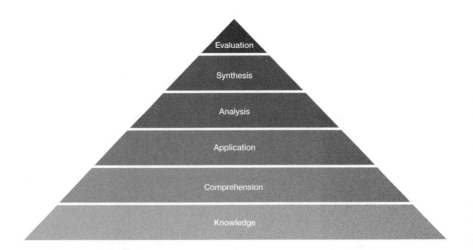

Figure 6.1 Bloom's Taxonomy of the Cognitive Domain

- *Knowledge*—involves the recall of specifics and universals, the recall of methods and procedures, or the recall of a pattern, structure or setting . . . the recall situation involves little more than bringing to mind the appropriate material (p. 201)
- *Comprehension*—the lowest level of comprehension. It refers to a type of understanding or apprehension such that the individual knows what is being communicated and can make use of the material or idea being communicated without necessarily relating it to other material or seeing its fullest implications (p. 204)
- *Application*—the use of abstractions in particular and concrete situations (p. 205)
- *Analysis*—the breakdown of a communication into its constituent elements or parts such that the relative hierarchy of ideas is made clear and/or the relations between the ideas expressed are made explicit (p. 205)
- *Synthesis*—the putting together of elements and parts so as to form a whole (p. 206)
- *Evaluation*—judgments about the value of materials and methods for given purposes (p. 207)

Figure 6.2 Bloom's Taxonomy Defined

For over five decades, educators have used Bloom's Taxonomy of the Cognitive Domain to plan instruction, to individualize lessons for students, and to support learning. In the context of close reading, you can use this system to provide consistent scaffolding of student cognition. Each cycle will not only encourage a careful re-reading of the text but also a measured deepening of thinking about its content. Thus, your instructional focus lays not in the simple understanding of the text but, more significantly, in the development of analytical thinking skills and critical analysis of the text.

The Bloom's Taxonomy Aligned to Close Reading table (Figure 6.3) delineates each classification level along with question stems and tasks. This chart can serve as a menu for you to prepare your close reading lesson. Simply select the question stem or task that is appropriate to your text and with each question/task systematically increase the degree of cognition needed to respond.

Taxonomy Level	Question Stems From Bloom's Verbs	Tasks Correlated to Bloom's Levels
Low-Level Cognition—Reading Cycle 1		
Knowledge	Find an example of ___. Name the main character. Identify ___. Describe ___. What is ___? Define ___. State the meaning of the word ___. List ___ from the text. Who . . . What . . . Where . . . When . . .? (from the text) Tell what happened in the text.	Chart Circle Code Draw Label Locate Highlight Outline Underline
Comprehension	Distinguish between ___ and ___. Explain why ___ happened? Indicate why you believe ___ happened. Interpret ___'s actions. Restate the text in your own words. Summarize the text.	Annotate Demonstrate Dramatize Sketch
Intermediate-Level Cognition—Reading Cycle 2		
Application	Using textual details, predict what would happen if ___. Give the main idea of the text. Explain how ___. What questions would you ask about ___? What examples from the text can you find about ___? What facts support the idea that ___? How would you organize the information from the text to illustrate ___? How ___? Why ___?	Demonstrate Diary Diorama Illustrate Journal Map Construct a model Perform Present Scrapbook Interview
Analysis	What conclusion can you draw from ___? How is ___ related to ___? Arrange ___ by common characteristics. Classify ___ into groups. Compare ___ and ___. Contrast ___ and ___. Differentiate between ___ and ___. Discriminate between ___ and ___. Distinguish between ___ and ___. What caused ___ to happen? Identify the parts of ___. What details support the conclusion that ___?	Chart Diagram Flowchart Venn diagram T-Chart Mobile

Figure 6.3 Bloom's Taxonomy Aligned to Close Reading

High-Level Cognition—Reading Cycle 3

| Synthesis | Arrange the author's reasons from most important to least important. Combine the authors' evidence into one argument. What is the lesson (theme) of the story? Explain how you would describe the character in this story. Hypothesize what you believe might have taken place if ___ occurred. Imagine how the outcome might change if ___. Rewrite the story ending. | Poem Advertisement Media product Cartoon Collage Design Create game Create song Write a newspaper article Pantomime Video Panel discussion |
| Evaluation | Argue against ___ by using the information from the text. Assess how well the author supported his argument. Decide if the author made an effective argument. Evaluate the author's use of ___. Compare two (or more) texts. Which one is better? Why? | Review of the text Panel discussion (to discuss effectiveness of text) Newspaper editorial Debate |

Figure 6.3 continued

The Bloom's Taxonomy Aligned to Close Reading figure presents a list of options from which to choose to develop a close reading lesson plan for the specific purpose of deepening student thinking and increasing academic rigor. The chart ranks the levels into three categories by Low-Level Cognition (Knowledge and Comprehension), Intermediate-Level Cognition (Application and Analysis), and High-Level Cognition (Synthesis and Evaluation). Simply follow the first reading cycle of the close reading with a Low-Level Cognition question or task. Likewise, the second reading cycle aligns to an Intermediate-Level Cognition question or task. By the third reading cycle, the scaffolding process prepares students to engage in High-Level Cognition with an appropriate question or task. The chart supplies a set of choices from which to choose, with each additional selection adding another dimension to the higher-order-thinking skills embedded in your instruction. Below is an example of a Bloom's Taxonomy Close Reading Framework.

CLOSE READING FRAMEWORK

BLOOM'S TAXONOMY

Step 1:   Identify the text.
Choose a text.

Step 2:   Determine purpose for reading.
To increase the rigor of student cognition when reading

Step 3:   Choose a model.
Bloom's Taxonomy

Step 4:   Decide how students will access texts.
Shared reading/Small-group reading/Paired reading

Step 5:   Complete first cycle of reading and present question/task.
Task: Code each of the parts of the story (narrative elements) C = Character, Se = Setting, P = Problem, and S = Solution. (Low-Level Cognition)

Step 6:   Provide time for discussion.
Ask students to retell the story using these coded narrative elements from the story to help them.

Step 7:   Complete second cycle of reading and present question/task.
Task: Write a journal entry through the point of view of the main character as he/she attempts to solve the problem in the story. (Intermediate-Level Cognition)

Step 8:   Provide time for discussion.
Encourage students to share their journal entries, and challenge them to validate their entries based on textual evidence from the story.

Step 9:   Complete third cycle of reading and present question/task.
Question: Evaluate how believable the character and his/her actions are in this story. (High-Level Cognition)

Step 10: Provide time for discussion.
Conduct a panel discussion eliciting from students textual details to support their arguments.

Webb's DOK Levels

In the 1990s, Norman Webb from the Wisconsin Center for Educational Research engineered Depths of Knowledge (DOK) Levels as a means to align standards and standardized assessments. He defined alignment as "the degree to which standards and assessments are in agreement and serve in conjunction with one another to guide the system toward students learning what they are expected to know and do" (Webb, 1997a, p. 3). Based on this view, his DOK model represents a scale of cognitive demand, reflecting the mental processing required to complete a task—emphasizing not the difficulty of the task itself but the thinking skills required to meet the intended outcomes.

"Expectations and assessments that are aligned will demand equally high learning standards for all students, while providing fair means for all students to demonstrate the expected level of learning." (Webb, 1997b, n.p.)

Devised in four levels, each tier amasses greater cognitive complexity, which allows educators to look at increasing rigor through the lens of content objectives, instruction, questions, tasks, and student outcomes. In effect, rigor can be calibrated through multiple contexts to ensure that student cognition deepens naturally and logically.

The model is both inclusive and progressive in nature so that later levels not only incorporate the skills and applications of earlier levels but also, more significantly, learners cannot progress until first mastering these earlier levels. What this means instructionally is that students should not move directly into DOK Level 4 until advancing through DOK Levels 1, 2, and 3 (Figure 6.4).

Level 1: Recall and Reproduction. Tasks at this level focus on "the recall of information such as a fact, definition, term, or a simple procedure" (Webb, 1999, p. 22). Within the context of reading, it only necessitates readers to be able to construct literal comprehension at the most basic level with just one cognitive step and one correct answer, which can be identified directly from the text. Questions and tasks from this level embody a shallow knowledge of the material.

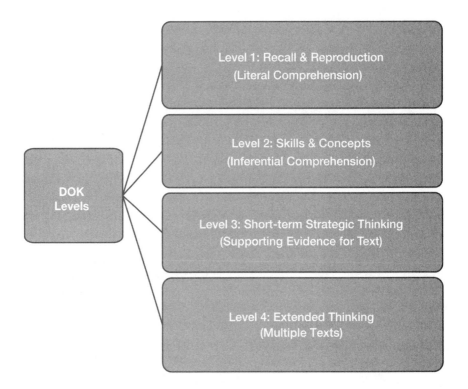

Figure 6.4 Webb's DOK Levels

- ◆ Identify the main character from the story.
- ◆ List the main events in the text.

Level 2: Skills and Concepts. This level "includes the engagement of some mental processing beyond a habitual response" (Webb, 1999, p. 22). It also places specific emphasis on inferential comprehension, which demands two or more cognitive steps.

- ◆ How would you describe the narrator's tone?
- ◆ What is the author's purpose in writing this text?

Level 3: Short-Term Strategic Thinking. Cognition deepens at this level, which "requires reasoning, planning, using evidence, and a higher level of thinking than the previous two levels. In most instances, requiring students to explain their thinking is a Level 3" (Webb, 1999, p. 22). This expectation will oblige the readers to use multiple cognitive steps with more than one correct answer. Using more abstract thinking, they must also be able to support their thinking with specific support from the text.

♦ How might the story have ended differently? Use evidence from the text to support your answer.

♦ How effective is the author's argument? Include details from the text to support your answer.

Level 4: Extended Thinking. This highest level of DOK represents readers' most rigorous and focused examination of text as well as their deepest extension in thinking. Level 4 "requires complex reasoning, planning, developing, and thinking most likely over an extended period of time. The extended period of time is not a distinguishing factor if the required work is only repetitive and does not require significant conceptual understanding and higher-order thinking" (Webb, 1999, pp. 22–23).

An inherent expectation is that students will have extended time with multiple sources to apply their understanding in real-life applications in new and different contexts.

♦ How does the theme differ between these two stories?

♦ What do the three texts suggest about ___?

Using the Webb's DOK Levels Aligned to Close Reading (Figure 6.5), you can create a close reading lesson plan utilizing four reading cycles. Following the first reading cycle, begin at Level 1 and select a question or task that initiates your students' literal comprehension of the text. Building on that foundation, move to Level 2, supporting your students' inferential understanding through appropriate questions or tasks. By the third reading cycle, students should be prepared to think about the text strategically, citing evidence to support their thinking. If you want your students to examine more than one text, Level 4 offers questions and tasks that will support their analysis and evaluation of multiple sources.

DOK Level	Close Reading Question Stems	Tasks
Level 1 Recall and Reproduction (Literal Comprehension)	Define the term ___. Tell what happened in the text. Identify ___. Can you define ___? Describe ___. When did ___ happen? What is ___? What is the meaning of ___?	Code the text. Create a timeline. Draw a circle, box, triangle around key information. Highlight important details. Label key details. Locate facts. Sequence the events.
Level 2 Skills and Concepts (Inferential Comprehension)	How was the word ___ used in the text? What is the main idea of this text? What is the moral (theme) of the story? Can you explain why ___ happened? What can you conclude about ___? How would you classify ___? Compare ___ and ___. How are they the same? Contrast ___ and ___. How are they different? Summarize the text. Why do you think ___ happened? What caused ___ to happen?	Circle the author's main argument. Annotate the passage, noting what interpretations you are making about the text. Draw a picture summarizing the text. Demonstrate what the text explained. Write a brief diary entry from the point of view of the author/character.
Level 3 Short-Term Strategic Thinking (Supporting Evidence)	What conclusion can you draw from ___? Use details from the text to support your answer. What facts support ___? What do you believe the author's purpose was for this text? Use textual evidence to support your answer. What do you predict will happen next? Why? How did the character change throughout the story? Be specific. Was the author's argument effective? Why? Was the author's conclusions supported by evidence?	Underline the reasons that the author gives to support his argument. Number each piece of evidence that supports the author's reasons. Construct a mobile which shows ___. Participate in a panel discussion. Participate in a short debate about ___. Be prepared to defend your position.
Level 4 Extended Thinking (Using Multiple Texts)	Analyze the texts. How are they different? How are they similar? Which text is most effective? Why? What do the texts suggest to you? Which texts support ___? How were the lessons (themes) between these two stories similar? Different? Compare both the primary source and secondary source, how are they similar and different?	Create a chart highlighting the similarities and differences between the texts. Draft an essay synthesizing the text's explanation. Construct a diagram describing ___. Write an editorial suggesting ___. Be certain to use evidence from the texts.

Figure 6.5 Webb's DOK Levels Aligned to Close Reading

CLOSE READING FRAMEWORK

Webb's DOK LEVELS

Step 1:   Identify the text.
Choose a text that warrants a rigorous examination.

Step 2:   Determine purpose for reading.
To increase the rigor of student cognition when reading

Step 3:   Choose a model.
DOK Levels

Step 4:   Decide how students will access texts.
Shared reading/Shared reading/Shared reading

Step 5:   Complete first cycle of reading and present question/task.
Question: What is the meaning of ___? (DOK Level 1)

Step 6:   Provide time for discussion.
Refer back to the text, drawing student attention to the clearly-defined term.

Step 7:   Complete second cycle of reading and present question/task.
Question: Why do you think ___ happened? (DOK Level 2)

Step 8:   Provide time for discussion.
Stress the importance of using evidence to make a text-based inference.

Step 9:   Complete third cycle of reading and present question/task.
Question: What conclusion can you draw from ___? Use details from the text to support your answer. (DOK Level 3)

Step 10: Provide time for discussion.
Reinforce the importance of supporting evidence when thinking deeply about text.

Step 11: Complete fourth cycle of reading and present question/task.
Question: What do the texts suggest to you? (DOK Level 4)

Step 12: Provide time for discussion.
Remind students to look for commonalities and differences between texts.

Comparing Bloom's Taxonomy and Webb's DOK Levels

At the essence of these two models remains their most significant difference. Bloom's Taxonomy utilizes a classification system as a means to promote higher order thinking skills, while Webb refers to his model as "nominative" and employs what could be considered a range of cognitive complexity. More specifically, Bloom centers on the learning outcome, or product. Conversely, Webb emphasizes the thinking skills process (Figure 6.6).

The models also differ significantly in their use of verbs. In Bloom's Taxonomy, the verbs represent the different classification tiers. In contrast, the learning outcome following the verb determines the DOK level. In effect, it is not the verb, but the context in which the verb is used, that indicates the DOK level. For example, consider the verb *describe*.

Level 1: *Describe* the character in the story.

Requires only recall of the facts presented in the text

Level 2: *Describe* the differences between the protagonist and antagonist.

Requires inferential thinking

Level 3: *Describe* how the character develops over the course of the story.

Requires connections and the development of generalizations among portions of the text with evidence to support thinking

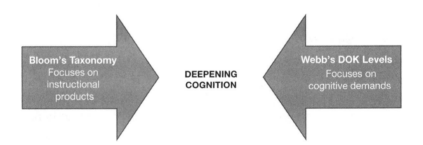

Figure 6.6 Comparison of Bloom's Taxonomy and Webb's DOK Levels

Bloom's Taxonomy		Webb's DOK Levels
Knowledge Comprehension	→	Level 1: Recall and Reproduction
Analysis	→	Level 2: Skills and Concepts
Application	→	Level 3: Strategic Thinking
Synthesis Evaluation	→	Level 4: Extended Thinking

Figure 6.7 Correlation of Bloom's Taxonomy and Webb's DOK Levels

Level 4: *Describe* how the character in this story is similar to or different from the character from the previous story.

Requires extended thinking across multiple texts

The two models cannot be neatly aligned; however, overlapping does occur between them (see Figure 6.7). DOK Level 1 requires basic recall, which roughly corresponds to Bloom's Knowledge and Comprehension. Level 2's expectation for inferential thinking equates to Analysis. Level 3 calls for strategic thinking and reasoning, which can also be found in Application. The extended thinking used in Level 4 parallels the cognition of Synthesis and Evaluation.

Differentiating Academic Rigor

Increasing academic rigor must be a primary goal of quality instruction. Using the question stems and tasks from Bloom's Taxonomy or Webb's DOK Levels, you can easily increase your instructional rigor and deepen your students' cognition through aligning the reading cycles with the appropriate levels. Using the Bloom's Taxonomy model, you would ask a Knowledge or Comprehension question/task after the first reading cycle, an Analysis or Application question/ task after the second reading cycle, and a Synthesis or Evaluation question/task after the third reading cycle. Likewise, you can focus students' understanding of the text with the first reading cycle with a DOK Level 1 Recall and Reproduction question/stem, a DOK Level 2 Skills and Concepts question/stem following the second reading cycle, and a DOK Level 3 Strategic Thinking question/stem with the third reading cycle. As an extension, if students have two or more texts relevant to the topic, students can follow with a DOK Level 4 Extended Thinking question/stem. In following the Bloom's Taxonomy Model or the DOK Model, your purpose (Step 2 from the Close Reading Framework) for the lesson centers on increasing instructional rigor.

We must also be cognizant that our students are not all identical to one another. They are, instead, unique with their own individual strengths and weaknesses. They come to our classrooms with different reading levels, aptitudes, and motivations. As much as close reading will level the playing field for students, differentiation continues to play a significant role in effective literacy instruction.

In the case of increasing academic rigor, providing multiple ways to make meaning from text offers a significant channel to differentiate the learning process. One of the most direct approaches for this is to create a Close Reading Menu. The menu provides a list of options when completing each reading cycle. Students can select the way in which they prefer to interact with the text, or you can choose for them based on their individual needs. You also have the option of placing students in groups and having them work collaboratively so that each member of the team has the same question or task as in the jigsaw activity described in Chapter 3. You might also diversify the questions and tasks beyond the standard expectation of one for the entire class, posing multiple questions or tasks within a given reading cycle, and then discussing with students how they responded, expanding their thinking yet again about a common text. You can even mix and match the item selections to include a variety of questions and tasks. Whatever design you create, you will increase rigor by incorporating all of these experiences into your follow-up discussion, thus, everyone shares regardless of the way in which they interact with the text. This can be a powerful mode of instruction as students not only learn from their own personal work with the text but also gain from others' work with the same text. In effect, encouraging students to share allows everyone to learn from each other.

This first example follows Bloom's Taxonomy levels (see Figure 6.8). Each level links to the cognitive difficulty associated with the question. Knowledge and Comprehension represent low-level cognitive skills. Application and Analysis reflect intermediate-level thinking, and the Synthesis and Evaluation levels constitute advanced-level thinking. You can decide to differentiate questions and tasks at the combined levels, or you can differentiate further through all six. Whatever format you select, you can offer students a range of options based on skill level, aptitude, or choice.

The DOK menu in Figure 6.9 utilizes both tasks and questions. Students can select which option they would like when reading the text. You can also make the decision, dividing the class into half with some students completing the task and others responding to the question. The subsequent discussion time would allow students to gain from both approaches, increasing their understanding of the text as well as potential strategies they may use independently when confronted with rigorous text.

The next example in Figure 6.10 represents a DOK menu with task choices aligned to multiple learning modalities. The choices range from simple highlighting and sketching for visual learners, to debates for those with auditory strengths, to mobiles and diagrams for students who learn best by being kinesthetically involved in the learning. They can select or you can suggest—either way students are engaging with text in ways conducive for their learning styles.

This last menu in Figure 6.11 allows for greater freedom in how students engage with text and would be more appropriate for upper elementary students who have experience with close reading lessons. With this menu, they determine what they will label, outline, bullet, highlight, etc. Thus, the lesson builds from their meaningful connections with the text. As always, the discussions following their text interactions remain crucial. They need to share what they labeled, bulleted, outlined, highlighted and why. This type of close reading lesson permits you to release responsibility for learning to your students, transitioning from a teacher-directed lesson while still maintaining a structured, supportive environment. It also compels students to be

1st Reading Low-Level Cognition		2nd Reading Intermediate-Level Cognition		3rd Reading Advanced-Level Cognition	
Knowledge	Comprehension	Application	Analysis	Synthesis	Evaluation
Define the term ___.	Distinguish between ___ and ___.	What questions would you ask about ___?	What are some of the problems of ___?	Arrange the author's reasons from most important to least important.	Argue against ___ by using the information from the text.
Tell what happened in the text.	Summarize the text.	Would this argument work in another situation?	Compare ___ and ___.	Combine the authors' evidence into one common argument.	Assess how well the author supported his argument.
Describe ___.	Explain why ___ happened.	Could this have happened if ___?	What caused ___ to happen?	Imagine a different outcome than the one in the text. What would have happened?	Is there a better outcome than the one described in the text?

Figure 6.8 Bloom's Taxonomy Menu

1st Reading Cycle Recall and Reproduction	2nd Reading Cycle Skills and Concepts	3rd Reading Cycle Strategic Thinking	4th Reading Cycle Extended Thinking
Draw a circle around ___.	Circle the author's main argument.	Underline the reasons the author listed to support his argument.	Create a chart highlighting the evidence the texts used to support their arguments.
What is the meaning of ___?	What is the main argument of the text?	Was the author's argument effective? Why?	Which text is most effective? Why?

Figure 6.9 DOK Menu Differentiated by Tasks and Questions

Modality	1st Reading Cycle Task: Recall and Reproduction	2nd Reading Cycle Task: Skills and Concepts	3rd Reading Cycle Task: Strategic Thinking	4th Reading Cycle Task: Extended Thinking
Visual	Code the text.	Draw a picture summarizing the text.	Underline the reasons that the author gives to support his argument.	Write an editorial suggesting ___. Be certain to use evidence from the texts.
Auditory	Retell the text to a partner.	Interview a partner to find out ___.	Participate in a short debate about ___. Be prepared to defend your position.	Write and perform a song which highlights the similarities and differences between the two texts.
Kinesthetic	Construct a diagram describing ___.	Demonstrate what the text explained.	Construct a mobile which shows ___.	Create a media product explaining ___ from the texts.

Figure 6.10 DOK Menu Differentiated by Learning Modality

1st Reading Cycle Task: Recall and Reproduction	2nd Reading Cycle Task: Skills and Concepts	3rd Reading Cycle Task: Strategic Thinking	4th Reading Cycle Task: Extended Thinking
Label	Illustrate	Chart	Story
Outline	Demonstrate	Mobile	Song
Bullet	Journal	Panel discussion	Editorial
Highlight	Reflect	Debate	Game

Figure 6.11 DOK Task Menu

active readers, cognizant of how they learn and the strategies they use to help them with complex text.

The example menus provided in this chapter offer some suggestions for the potential in elevating literacy instruction in the classroom in an intentional, well planned way. By progressing through the levels using any of these cognitive models, you scaffold students as they delve deeper into text and expand their thinking about content. These models can also be used for differentiating individual students to meet them where they are as they develop their skills. What's more, students can be grouped together, sharing the same level question/task, which promotes collaboration and peer-to-peer support. Following the range of question/tasks utilized through the menu comes the whole-group discussion. This point further deepens students' thinking as they share their own experiences with the text and learn additional information from their classmates, thus augmenting their understanding through a variety of avenues. In essence, any configuration you select will increase student cognition and their interaction with challenging text.

Chapter Summary

Close reading provides a supportive framework for scaffolding student understanding of complex text as well as for specific instructional purposes like examining literary genres or developing particular comprehension skills. As beneficial as the strategy remains for these goals, close reading should not be overlooked for its capacity to raise the level of rigor in classroom instruction and to deepen student cognition when interacting with text.

Since 1956, educators have used Bloom's Taxonomy to elevate the level of tasks that they pose to students. Using this classification system, instruction can target individual levels with the intent of progressing to increasing degrees of difficulty. Four decades later, Norman Webb developed Depth of Knowledge (DOK) Levels to align standards and assessments, ensuring that educators were aware of how standards, curriculum instruction, and assessment work in tandem to deliver expected student outcomes, which focus on the thinking skills necessary to achieve them. Pairing these cognitive models with close reading sets forth a novel approach to increase rigor in the classroom.

Rigor, however, does not signify identical expectations for all students. The reality is that what may be rigorous for some students will not be for others. The scope of instruction needed to support rigor across an entire classroom can be daunting and, frankly, overwhelming. Differentiating rigor offers a simple remedy for this problem. Using a menu from which students, or you, can select proves to be even more straightforward—un-complicating an otherwise challenging situation.

Book Study

Reflection Questions

Chapter 6: Reading with Increasing Levels of Rigor

1. How are Bloom's Taxonomy and Webb's DOK Levels similar?

2. How are they different?

3. When do you visualize using a Bloom's Taxonomy or DOK Close Reading Model? Why?

4. How else could you differentiate students' cognition?

5. *TASK*: Craft a close reading lesson using Bloom's Taxonomy and then Webb's DOK Levels as a classification for increasing rigor. How are they similar? How are they different? Which one do you prefer? Why?

Part III

Linking Close Reading with Close Talks and Close Writes

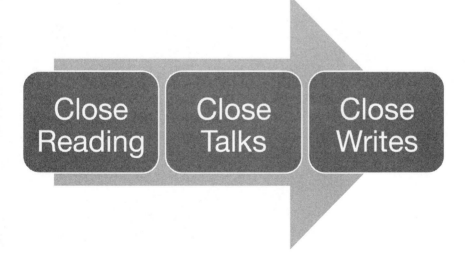

7

Using Close Talks to Deepen Understanding

A close talk is a purposeful, focused discussion about a brief text(s) with the goal of deepening student understanding of the content as well as increasing the ability to participate in academic discussions. This discussion only occurs after a close reading lesson and is designed as a natural progression to scaffold student cognition. Although it works in tandem with close reading, close talk derives philosophically from the work of Socrates.

Born in 470 BC, Socrates was a Greek philosopher from whom much of American educational pedagogy rests. Socrates believed that learning occurred not from lecture but rather emerged from disciplined conversation.

Socrates' theory, referred to as the dialectic method, or more simply understood as a structured discussion for the purpose of intellectual investigation, called on learners not only to discuss content but also to examine what they know, to question the validity of the

"Communication is an essential part of the learning processes itself, which is to say that students learn by communicating (and do not engage in communication only after they have achieved mastery over the learning material)." (Kühnen et al., 2012, p. 60)

content, and to gather meaning from sharing with others. Socrates asserted that questioning students was the only authentic form of teaching and that the goal of education should be for students to think for themselves.

He commonly began his teaching by posing a problem to his students then encouraged them to clarify their understanding of the topic. Believing that student understanding can be nurtured by progressively correcting inaccurate assumptions or notions until they reach a complete, accurate grasp of the material, he chose not to affirm their answers, but instead, he responded with further questions as a means to elicit meaningful thinking and reflection.

The Socratic method became popular in Europe during the Enlightenment. It eventually migrated to the United States as a counterpoint to the nation's dependence on lecture and rote recall. Its prevalence became even more entrenched in the 1920s when the Great Books movement swept throughout the country and with it the creation of the Socratic seminar.

The purpose of the Socratic seminar is to engage students in critical analysis through generative questions that naturally propel both dialogue and cognition. In the course of the discussion, students rationalize their thinking process and their responses. Collaborative in nature, the facilitator (teacher) carefully plans the questions to guide students to an end learning goal.

Developed later, Socratic circles embody a more structured application of methodology in which text becomes the central focal point. Although variations exist, typically students first read a common text during which they gain a basic understanding of its meaning. On the day of the seminar, the class forms two concentric circles—one inside the other. The inner circle begins to probe the text for deeper meaning and intent with the outer circle critiquing the quality of their discussion. Then, the circles switch places with the outer circle moving to the center and discussing the text while the inner circle moves outside to observe the dialogue.

Both of these methods rest on the work of Socrates' emphasis on the power of questions to advance student understanding in specific content as well as student thinking in general. Even in the absence of these discussion models, questioning remains the primary way we instruct our students and ascertain their understanding of content.

The Power of Questioning

The majority of instructional time in classrooms is devoted to asking questions. Teachers ask from 300–400 questions a day (Levin & Long, 1981). With 180 school days in an academic year, that indicates 72,000 questions annually or over the course of a K-12 educational experience 936,000 questions. That suggests nearly a million opportunities to engage students in critical thinking and reflective analysis of content. Unfortunately, numerous studies have investigated the quality of classroom questioning and have found that up to 80 percent of these questions reflect factual recall of the text and lower-level cognitive inquiry (Cohn & Kottkamp, 1993; Flippione, 1998 as cited in Crowe & Stanford, 2010; USDOE, 1980). In fact, it pervades instructional practice as research has found that classrooms emphasize "copying, remembering and reciting with few tasks that engage students in thinking about what they have read" (Allington, 2001, p. 94).

Although both research and conventional wisdom indicate that frequent questioning has a causal effect on student achievement (Good & Brophy, 2000), it is the quality of questions—not the quantity —that serves to increase student learning outcomes. Thus, utilizing the power of Socratic methodology provides greater opportunities not only to ask questions but also, and more importantly, to ask questions that matter, that encourage divergent, creative thinking, and that build active, independent readers.

Close Talks

Close talks link the reading process with dialogue in a supportive environment as students use the knowledge they have garnered from close reading to launch their own analysis of the content into more meaningful pathways. Just as with close reading, you must carefully plan for a close talk with a distinct purpose in mind, carefully select text(s), and construct backward-designed student questions.

While the Socratic method shapes the philosophical under-pinnings of close talk, close talks offer a unique framework for student engagement with the text. First, it works in tandem with close reading as an extension and deepening of critical thinking skills. Second, in contrast to other Socratic methodologies, the teacher does not function as a facilitator but, instead, monitors the discussion, slipping in and out of the dialogue as needed to clarify concepts. Third, although the questions are meant to be generative in nature, the teacher designs a three- to five-item question guide through which students work collaboratively to engage in critical inquiry of the text. The benefits are summarized in Figure 7.1 and explained in more detail later in this chapter.

To ensure the effectiveness of a close talk, begin with four building blocks: text, questions, students, and teacher (Figure 7.2). Each component constitutes an essential element of classroom dialogue.

Text

The first step is to choose an appropriate text. Just as with selecting a text for close reading, a text for a close talk should be challenging and thought-provoking, providing students an authentic context from which to construct meaning at a deeper level in a way that may not happen in the natural occurrence of classroom instruction. While it may come from fiction, nonfiction, poetry, illustrations/photographs, websites, etc., it should be relatively brief so that students can manage

---

♦ encourages critical reading of text
♦ scaffolds student understanding of complex text
♦ creates a community of learners
♦ provides time for deep analysis of content
♦ fosters a constructivist classroom
♦ ensures active learning
♦ increases student engagement
♦ aids internalization of skills and content knowledge
♦ develops the thinking necessary for the writing process.

Figure 7.1 Benefits of Close Talks

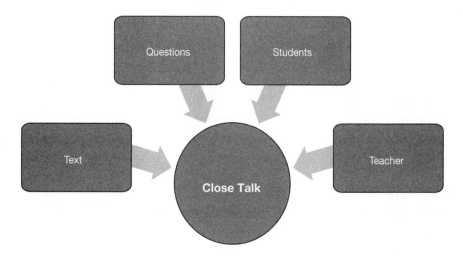

Figure 7.2 Components of a Close Talk

the content at the literal level before embarking on more complex thinking about the topic. It should also support multiple viewpoints so that students can consider the text from different perspectives.

Questions

Questions form the foundation of an effective close talk. Selecting questions at the literal level will lead you on the path of a rapid fire question-answer volley between you and your students. The power of a close talk is its potential to engage students in sustained, layered thinking about text within the environment of a classroom discussion.

For a close talk of 30–45 minutes, prepare three to five questions to guide the discussion. The initial question should launch the talk, necessitate students to refer back to the text, and generate further conversation. As students delve through the layered meanings, subsequent questions should follow a logical sequence that moves thinking and discussion toward more critical analysis and evaluation. To support the process, questions should concentrate on a number of key attributes: intentional queries, expansive discussion, divergent thinking, and text-dependent support. Sample questions representing a range of thinking stems are shown in Figure 7.3.

Intentional queries. Questions must be carefully crafted to scaffold students' understanding about a given concept. Close talks should have a purpose, and this purpose should be reflected clearly within the questions posed to students. More specifically, each question should progress in a deliberate, intentional manner to a designated student learning expectation. This allows you to target a learning outcome and direct student thinking and discussion toward that target.

Divergent thinking. Avoid convergent, closed questions with only one correct answer as this will stifle the discussion and subvert student attention from more rigorous analysis of the text. Instead, construct open-ended questions that support more than a simple right or wrong response.

Expansive discussion. Recognizing the need for a layered analysis and reflection of the text, questions should open the possibilities of how students may think about, respond, and react to others. Questions should encourage students to develop their own insights, build off the thoughts and ideas of others, and be able to link ideas inherent in a class discussion.

Text-dependent support. Questions should necessitate students referring back to the text, searching for evidence to substantiate their thinking. With the goal for students to become independent, critical learners, they must, within this course of action, be skilled in how to construct knowledge from the text and be cognizant of its intent.

Students

The students must have had sufficient time to examine the text and reach, at the very least, a literal understanding of its meaning. Conducting a close reading lesson prior to a close talk will ensure that they have the necessary comprehension and appreciation of the text to participate in the discussion.

Before beginning, review the protocol to clarify both their responsibilities and the format for the discussion. They should be aware that they will need to substantiate their responses through textual evidence, to examine the text further, and to pose their own individual questions as the dialogue continues.

QUESTIONS

Interpretive

♦ Why do you think ___ happened?

♦ What lesson can we learn from this story?

♦ What is the theme of this story?

♦ What do you believe is the main idea of this text?

♦ What do you think the purpose of this text is? Why?

♦ How would you describe ___?

♦ How are ___ and ___ similar?

♦ How are ___ and ___ different?

♦ Why do you think ___ happened?

♦ What does ___ mean?

♦ How are these two texts alike/unlike?

♦ Would changing the point of view also change the story?

♦ Does the illustration/picture/photograph change the way you think about the text?

♦ What would you include in a summary of this text?

♦ What is the most important word/phrase/sentence in the text?

Evaluative

♦ Does the author have sufficient reasons to support his argument?

♦ Is the evidence used by the author credible?

♦ Do you think that the author organizes his/her reasons in the most effective way to support the argument? Why or why not?

♦ How can you refute the author's argument?

Clarifying

♦ Why do you say that?

♦ Can you explain what you mean by that?

♦ What evidence from the text supports your answer?

♦ How does this connect to what we have discussed before?

♦ What does that tell us about the text?

Focusing

♦ How does this relate to our conversation?

♦ Can you find evidence from the text to support your thoughts?

Figure 7.3 Close Talk Question Stems

During the close talk, students should listen respectfully to others, waiting politely before entering the conversation. When responding, they need to demonstrate their understanding of the text by utilizing a mixture of literal recall of text details, inferential thinking about the content, and an evaluative stance to appraise the quality of the material. Citing textual details also becomes an integral asset to provide support to their thinking. As students develop skills in participating in close talks, encourage them to build from others' comments, paraphrasing as a means to connect the discussion into a meaningful whole.

Teacher

Your role changes throughout this activity. Before engaging your students in a close talk, you must first select a text worthy of its time demands. As with close reading, it should be a text that is complex, challenging, and necessitates these added scaffolds to ensure that students truly understand its meaning and intent. Once chosen, you will find that completing a close reading lesson first will allow your students to gain a deeper grasp of the content—which will be essential for them to participate in the close talk. After explaining the protocol, they should be ready to begin!

Initiate the close talk by posing an open-ended, divergent question that should have multiple perspectives, which students may take in considering their responses. As they begin to converse, let the dialogue flow, stopping when necessary to encourage them to elaborate on their thinking, to clarify their positions, to correct inaccurate assumptions, or to re-focus the talk.

Preparing a Close Talk

Develop your own close talk by following the plan in Figure 7.4 for pre-, during-, and post-talk activities. During the pre-talk phase, complete a close reading of the text to ensure that students have the requisite surface knowledge to equip themselves for a thoughtful dialogue about the content. Then, use a backward design to develop

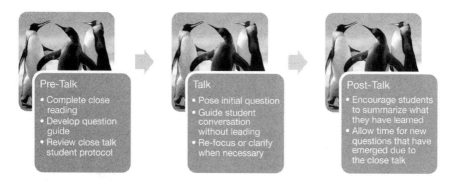

Figure 7.4 Close Talk Steps

a guide of three to five questions that will naturally advance students to the learning outcome you have set. Also, be certain to explain to your students about participating in a close talk—its purpose, the guidelines for their participation, and your role. During the close talk, pose your initial question. Be certain that it is open-ended, generative, and engaging. As students respond to the question and begin to develop an interactive dialogue with one another, let them direct the discussion, halting the discussion when necessary to clarify their thinking, to direct their understanding of their own cognitive process, or to re-focus the group if the discussion goes off task from the content. During the post-talk phase, provide time for a wrap-up of their learning by encouraging students to summarize what they are taking away from this activity. Also, encourage students to voice any additional questions that have arisen due to their class discussion.

Guidelines for Participating in a Close Talk

Prepare your students for participating in a close talk by teaching the following student-friendly protocol:

1. Be respectful to others when listening and speaking.
2. Refer back to the text to support your responses.

3. Connect your ideas and thoughts to what you have heard in the discussion.

4. Stay focused on the topic.

5. Be prepared to share what you have learned at the end of the close talk.

Close Talk Procedure

You can design and implement your own close talk by following six easy steps.

1. Read text prior to participating in close talk. Students bring text with them to the class discussion.

2. Teacher poses an opening question to begin class dialogue.

3. Students respond to question, sharing their own insights, citing textual evidence, and linking their ideas to those of their classmates.

4. Teacher enters the dialogue to elicit more rigorous thinking, clarify misconceptions about the content, encourage the citing of textual support, or re-focus the group discussion.

5. Teacher poses two or more additional questions that encourage deeper analysis.

6. The class summarizes their learning and debriefs the close talk process.

Close Talk Participation Rubric

The Close Talk Participation Rubric (Figure 7.5) should be displayed and discussed prior to any close talk activity. Aligned to the guidelines for participation, the rubric illustrates the developing stages that students may experience as they begin to participate in close talks. Beginning Talkers (Score 1) define the student who has not yet mastered the skills necessary to dialogue with others in a meaningful, academic way. This student may also experience difficulty with understanding the content and with sharing his/her understanding with others. Skilled Talkers (Score 2) describe the student who is gaining comfort in the protocols of the classroom discussion (e.g., listening to others, keeping pace with the flow of ideas, adding to the dialogue with appropriate comments or questions). Skilled Talkers also understand concepts of the text both literally and inferentially. Proficient Talkers (Score 3) have gained the capabilities of Skilled Talkers as well as being able to evaluate the text through deeper critical analysis and to cite textual evidence to support their contributions to the discussion. Reflective Talkers (Score 4) depict the student who has amassed the previous skills and can offer personal insights along with linking their ideas with those expressed by others, propelling the discussion forward.

Before conducting the first talk in your classroom, review the rubric with your students to help them become aware of the expectations. Then, assess them after the first close talk, meeting briefly with each student to assign a current score level and make recommendations

1—Beginning Talker	• Ignores discussion • Distracts others from talk • Demonstrates little understanding of the text • Responds with literal, surface-level understanding
2—Skilled Talker	• Listens respectfully • Follows discussion • Demonstrates some understanding of text • Responds with a mixture of literal and inferential understanding
3—Proficient Talker	• Listens respectfully • Engages in discussion • Demonstrates comprehensive understanding of text • Responds with a mixture of literal, inferential, and evaluative understanding • Cites text
4—Reflective Talker	• Listens respectfully • Moves discussion forward • Demonstrates deep understanding of text • Responds with a mixture of literal, inferential, and evaluative understanding • Cites text • Shares personal insights • Connects responses to others' comments

Figure 7.5 Close Talk Participant Rubric

for how to raise his/her close talk skills. As you continue to integrate close talks into your instructional practice, maintain brief student conferences and close talk debriefings to scaffold students toward the goal of becoming reflective readers and thinkers.

Benefits of Close Talk

The benefits of close talks exceed deep content learning and higher-order thinking skills to encompass essential skills of independent readers, writers, and thinkers.

♦ *Encourages critical reading of text*—Participating in a close talk necessitates students reading the focus text prior to the class discussion. In the midst of the discussion, the questions posed center on deeper levels of understanding.

♦ *Scaffolds student understanding of complex text*—The close talk is a continuation of the support system for students as they engage with text that they find challenging. It begins with the close reading lesson with each re-reading becoming progressively more focused on meaning and intent. Linking the close talk provides a structured, disciplined dialogue from which to continue to refine student thinking about content as well their understanding of the thinking process itself.

♦ *Creates a classroom of learners*—The nature of a close talk builds a sense of community as students work together to construct meaning, sharing their personal insights as well as learning from the thoughts and ideas of others in the classroom.

♦ *Provides time for deep analysis of content*—In the rush "to cover" content, a close talk sets aside protected time for students to read, think, reflect, and collaborate on a given text. It also communicates to students that taking time to think deeply about text has import, has value for good readers, and can—will—change the way we understand the meaning of a text.

♦ *Fosters a constructivist classroom*—In contrast to a teacher-centered classroom emphasizing one quickly-located right answer, close talk engenders a constructivist environment. In constructivist classrooms, the emphasis shifts to students, and it becomes their responsibility to build understanding for themselves when learning transitions into a more personalized approach to acquiring skills and content.

♦ *Ensures active learning*—This instructional activity shifts attention from teacher talk to student talk. Engaging in this student-led discourse demands that students listen actively to others, contribute their own understandings of the text, and connect their learning to that found from other texts, classmates, and their teacher.

♦ *Increases student engagement*—Engagement is generally recognized to be correlated to student achievement. One of the strengths of close talks centers in its ability to initiate student dialogue—benefitting from human nature's desire to work with others. Instead of reading and answering questions independently, they have the opportunity to read together, talk through the content, and answer questions collaboratively—building knowledge through many rather than one.

♦ *Aids internalization of skills and content knowledge*—Close talks allow students the time, practice, and support needed to think more deeply about content as well as their own thinking and how they process information. This repetition of skill-building (e.g., drawing conclusions, making connections among texts, searching for textual evidence) and analytical approach to content knowledge increases student internalization and mastery.

♦ *Develops the thinking necessary for the writing process*—A stumbling block in student-generated writing is the common refrain, "I don't know what to write!" Using close reading to delve into text followed by close talk to deepen critical analysis as well as to consider multiple viewpoints expressed by others furnishes a richer understanding of the content and develops a much greater supply of content knowledge from which students can draw for their own writing.

Chapter Summary

Close talks is an instructional activity that requires purposeful, recursive experiences with a short complex text as a foundation for academic-driven and text-dependent classroom discussion. Building on the learning theory of the Greek philosopher, Socrates, it emphasizes the act of questioning as a means for students to become actively engaged in making meaning and in critically analyzing the text.

Text, questions, students, and the teacher comprise the primary components of close talk. Each one functions as an essential link in the process of thinking and talking about texts. The text represents the foundation of the entire activity and must lend itself to repeated readings, reflective analysis, and extended class discussion. Just as with close reading, this activity demands a text worthy of its time and complex enough to warrant a sustained class discussion. Questions for the close talk should be rigorous, generative, and naturally progress to a predetermined learning outcome. To ensure its effectiveness, students should be aware of what is expected of them during this activity as well as the scoring rubric by which both you and they can assess their proficiency with content and academic discourse. The teacher, as with all rigorous instruction, plans out a close talk meticulously before beginning. The text must be selected; the close reading should be completed prior to the talk; a question guide must be crafted by a backward design that carefully supports student thinking about the content, and time needs to be scheduled to allow for student reflection and conferencing.

Book Study

Reflection Questions

Chapter 7: Using Close Talks to Deepen Understanding

1. How do academic conversations support learning in a classroom?

2. How do close talks build off Socrates' theory of learning?

3. What do you believe is the most significant benefit of close talks for students?

4. *TASK*: Plan a close talk for an upcoming text. Include the specific questions you will ask as well as how you can support your students in this initial experience with close talks.

8

Close Writes as a Springboard into Student-Generated Writing

In 2003, the National Commission on Writing released the seminal report, *The Neglected "R": The Need for a Writing Revolution,* arguing that writing had been neglected in deference to the necessity of reading instruction and making the powerful claim that "writing today is not a frill for the few, but an essential skill for the many" (p. 11).

Recognizing that writing is thinking made visible on paper (or in this technological society, on screen), the report stressed the urgency of writing as the "key to transforming learning in the United States" (p. 13).

A year later, the National Commission on Writing (2004) issued a second report—this time garnered from the results of a business roundtable consisting of 120 American corporations. Its findings indicated that writing is deemed a "threshold skill" for employment with half of the companies reporting that they consider applicants' writing skills when hiring, quoting one respondent as stating "writing could be your ticket in . . . or it could be your ticket out" (p. 3).

> *"If students are to make knowledge their own, they must struggle with the details, wrestle with the facts, and rework raw information and dimly understood concepts into language they can communicate to someone else. In short, if students are to learn, they must write." (National Commission on Writing, 2003, p. 9)*

As they continued their resolve to bring writing to the forefront of school reform, the National Commission on Writing reported again in 2006 that more than 80 percent of blue-collar workers and more than 90 percent of white-collar workers stated that writing is significant to their work success (as cited in Graham & Hebert, 2010). Despite the necessity of writing in daily life, only 1 percent of high school seniors can write an advanced, well-organized essay and up to 75 percent of students in grades 4 through 12 are characterized as poor writers (Tyre, 2012). Again and again, the call has come to recognize the significance of writing instruction in schools (Applebee & Langer, 2006; Gibson, 2008; Graham & Hebert, 2010; Troia & Olinghouse, 2013). Yet, little has changed in classrooms.

If the writing revolution envisioned by the National Commission on Writing and urged by so many literacy experts is to take place, the change begins in elementary schools. It is in these early years of foundational learning that writing must gain prominence (Graham et al., 2012) to develop the skills needed in secondary school, universities, and the job market.

Reading–Writing Connection

The focus on writing, however, still falters as public attention remains on the clamor over the literacy gap and the rush to raise reading achievement. To bridge this gap, one key to the solution is to embrace the reading–writing connection. Writing instruction does not simply improve writing. In studying one failing school in the state of New York, Tyre (2012) recounted that a consistent finding was that successful students could express their thinking on paper and failing students could not. Defined as "the connection, interplay, and mutual influence of reading and writing" (Harris & Hodges, 1995), the reading–writing connection is indisputable (Nelson & Calfee, 1998; Shanahan, 2006), sharing what noted reading researcher P. David Pearson refers to as "synergy." This symbiotic relationship centers on the cognitive processes that they both possess. While reading focuses on receptive thinking, and writing reflects more productive cognition, they both construct meaning and require specialized process skills. At the most foundational level, reading requires students to decode written text in order to gain understanding from symbols on a page. Conversely, writing necessitates students to encode those symbols to form meaningful words, sentences, and paragraphs. As literacy development continues, students read in order to learn about the world around them, while they write to express that learning in ways that are personal and unique to them.

This connection between reading and writing has been studied at length, and researchers have proven that writing instruction does indeed influence reading achievement (Graham & Hebert, 2010). Similarly, reading instruction demonstrates a positive impact of writing achievement (Krashen, 1993). Further evidence of their relationship manifests in student learning outcomes with incidence rates of written-language disorders and reading disabilities appearing to be similar (Katusic, Colligan, Weaver, & Barbaresi, 2009).

Fletcher and Portalupi (1998) asserted in their book, *Craft Lessons: Teaching Writing K-8*, that "literature may be the most crucial [influence] of all. The writing you get out of your students can only be as good as the literature that surrounds and sustains it. The writing classroom is built on the foundation of literature" (p. 10). While today's teachers have come to realize the importance of nonfiction text as well, the premise still rings true—good writing comes from quality texts.

Although schools have historically taught both reading and writing, they have traditionally been taught separately with no appreciation that these are complementary cognitive skill sets (see Figure 8.1). This continued until the 1970s and 1980s when research in the reading–writing connection began, and classroom instruction followed with educators integrating the two content areas.

If students are to benefit from this now accepted instructional strength of the reading–writing connection, we must be intentional and systemic in our approach. For example, *Writing to Read: Evidence for How Writing Can Improve Reading*, a report from the Carnegie Corporation (Graham & Hebert, 2010), recommended three clusters of writing practices that would improve reading. First, base student writing on the texts they read (e.g., summaries, notes, question responses). Second, provide explicit instruction on the writing skills and processes necessary to craft text (e.g., writing process, text structures, and paragraph construction). Third, increase the amount of student-generated writing.

Conceptualization of Reading	Conceptualization of Writing
1700s—Reading instruction based on the schooling concepts of the British primary model, using the Bible as an instructional text.	1700s—Writing instruction based on the rhetoric of Aristotle with emphasis on grammar and style.
1800s—Scientific experiments served as the basis for the theory of reading instruction.	1800s—The art of writing emerges.
Early 1900s—Reading instruction focused on psychological research; from 1940s–1960s, behavioral psychology dominated the field.	Early 1900s—Writing instruction focused on practical needs.
1970s—Cognitive psychology and constructivism gained prevalence.	1970s—Research into the complexities of writing flourishes.
1980s—Research into the reading–writing connection is born.	

Figure 8.1 Conceptualizations of Reading and Writing Domains

Source: Langer, J. A., & Flihan, S. (2000). Writing and reading relationships. In R. Indrisano and J. R. Squire (Eds.), *Perspectives on Writing: Research, Theory, and Practice*. Newark, DE: International Reading Association.

The Common Core State Standards architects have recognized both the undeniable strength of the reading–writing connection as well as the amazing potential it offers when used as two parts of a whole. This appreciation materializes in the blending of reading and writing standards as well as the standards' reliance on reading to develop writing skills.

So, writing instruction anchors literacy development, and yet its presence in classrooms is still negligible with writing achievement reflecting only rudimentary skills—a chasm between what students can currently do and what the expectations are for them in order to succeed academically and in life. How can educators begin to address the need for quality writing instruction? Close reading, or more appreciably, close writes.

The Close Write Model

The close write models provided in this text ground themselves in the research of quality writing instruction and the benefits of the reading–writing connection. They center on the selection of quality literary and informational texts as mentor texts for models of effective writing. Too often in classrooms, reading and writing are deemed separate and share no overlap of instruction, time, or appreciation. Using close reading techniques as a launch to student-generated writing serves to benefit from the reading–writing connection. Close writes follow the same pedagogical underpinnings of close reading in that they emphasize the importance of purposeful re-readings of short pieces of text to guide the reader into greater and greater understanding of complex text with the goal to analyze the text at a critical level searching for the text's meaning and intent. They do, however, use these re-readings to guide student understanding not just as readers but also as writers. Each reading directs student attention to key details upon which they will construct their own writing.

The close write model follows the ten-step framework described throughout the text as a scaffold to guide students not only to read with purpose and intent to analyze text but also to write from that text using incremental steps to analyze the written text before synthesizing their understanding in original writing pieces. At the conclusion of the close write, students will have the tangible ingredients needed for writing. For those students who struggle with basic composition, for those students who complain that they don't know what to write, and for those students who write fluently but falter in the presence of new writing tasks, close writes will provide the structured, step-by-step process they need to develop their confidence and writing skills in authentic ways.

CLOSE READING FRAMEWORK

BEGINNING NARRATIVES

Step 1:   Identify the text.
Choose a text that has strong narrative elements.

Step 2:   Determine purpose for reading.
To improve beginning narrative writing skills

Step 3:   Choose a model.
Narratives

Step 4:   Decide how students will access texts.
Paired reading/Paired reading/Paired reading

Step 5:   Complete first cycle of reading and present question/task.
Task: Circle the characters and setting of the story.
Working with a partner, begin to think of a new story with the same character(s) but a new setting. Write down which character(s) and in what new setting the story will take place.

Step 6:   Provide time for discussion.
Ask pairs to share which characters from the original text will be in their new story and what setting they have selected. Reinforce that the setting must be realistic to the first one.

Step 7:   Complete second cycle of reading and present question/task.
Task: Number the events in the story. Write a "P" above the problem in the story and an "S" above the solution of the story. Brainstorm the events of the new story to be written.

Step 8:   Provide time for discussion.
Remind students that the beginning of the story should set up the action. The middle should reflect the character(s)'s problem, and the end should provide closure for the solution of the problem. Encourage pairs to share their sequence of events, asking students to critique their classmates' story plan in a collaborative, respectful way. Emphasize that their stories need a clear beginning, middle, and end with a problem and a solution.

Step 9:   Complete third cycle of reading and present question/task.
Task: Underline all of the time words that show the sequence of the story events (e.g., first, next, then, finally). Write the appropriate time words beside the events for the new story to be written with arrows showing where they should go.

Step 10: Provide time for discussion.
Discuss the importance of time words to help the reader understand the order of the events. Brainstorm additional time words that the students can use. Use the student-generated story map as a scaffold for their narratives.

INTERMEDIATE NARRATIVES

Step 1:   Identify the text.
Choose a text that has strong narrative elements.

Step 2:   Determine purpose for reading.
To improve intermediate narrative writing skills

Step 3:   Choose a model.
Intermediate Narratives

Step 4:   Decide how students will access texts.
Paired reading/Paired reading/Paired reading

Step 5:   Complete first cycle of reading and present question/task.
Task: Circle the characters and setting of the story. Number the events in the story. Write a "P" above the problem in the story and an "S" above the solution of the story. Working with a partner, begin to think of a new story with the same character(s) but a new setting. Write down which character(s) and in what new setting the

story will take place as well as a numbered sequence of events. Place the problem (with a "P" over it) in one of the middle events. Place the solution (with an "S" over it) in one of the last events.

Step 6: Provide time for discussion.
Ask pairs to share their story map. Emphasize the need for a natural flow of events and a clear problem and solution with closure.

Step 7: Complete second cycle of reading and present question/task.
Task: Highlight the descriptive words and draw an arrow to what they are describing. Add descriptive words in blue beside the story elements in the story to be written— character(s), setting, events. Draw arrows to what they are describing.

Step 8: Provide time for discussion.
Emphasize that descriptive words make the story more interesting and gives the reader mental pictures of the characters, setting, and what is happening in the story.

Step 9: Complete third cycle of reading and present question/task.
Task: Draw a box around character dialogue. Create dialogue for the new story, and number each piece of dialogue to show to which event it belongs.

Step 10: Provide time for discussion.
Discuss how dialogue reveals information about characters and moves the story forward. Use the student-generated story map as a scaffold for their narratives.

CLOSE READING FRAMEWORK

ADVANCED NARRATIVES

Step 1: Identify the text.
Choose a text that has strong narrative elements.

Step 2: Determine purpose for reading.
To improve advanced narrative writing skills

Step 3: Choose a model.
Advanced Narratives

Step 4: Decide how students will access texts.
Paired reading/Paired reading/Paired reading

Step 5: Complete first cycle of reading and present question/task.
Task: Circle the characters and setting of the story.
Number the events in the story. Write a "P" above the problem in the story and an "S" above the solution of the story. Working with a partner, begin to think of a new story with the same character(s) but a new setting. Write down which character(s) and in what new setting the story will take place as well as a numbered sequence of events. Place the problem (with a "P" over it) in one of the middle events. Place the solution (with an "S" over it) in one of the last events.

Step 6: Provide time for discussion.
Ask pairs to share their story map. Emphasize the need for a natural flow of events and a clear problem and solution with closure.

Step 7: Complete second cycle of reading and present question/task.
Task: Draw a box around words and phrases that shift between time and settings. Write the appropriate transitional words and phrases between the numbered events.

Step 8: Provide time for discussion.
Stress how transitional words and phrases move time and place naturally. Brainstorm additional transitional terms.

Step 9: Complete third cycle of reading and present question/task.
Task: Highlight sensory language (e.g., words that help the reader see, hear, touch, taste, and hear the story). Brainstorm sensory language for the new story and label where it should go—characters, setting, problem, solution, or events.

Step 10: Provide time for discussion.
Emphasize that sensory language can make words on a page come to life. Brainstorm additional sensory language.
Use the student-generated story map as a scaffold for their narratives.

CLOSE READING FRAMEWORK

BEGINNING EXPOSITORY WRITING

Step 1: Identify the text.
Choose a text that contains a clear examination of a nonfiction topic.

Step 2: Determine purpose for reading.
To improve beginning expository writing

Step 3: Choose a model.
Beginning Expository Writing

Step 4: Decide how students will access texts.
Paired reading/Paired reading/Paired reading

Step 5: Complete first cycle of reading and present question/task.
Task: Circle the topic of the text. Using a simplified writing map, write Topic and list the topic of the text.

Step 6: Provide time for discussion.
Discuss the topic of the text, reinforcing that the topic should be introduced at the beginning of an informational text.

Step 7: Complete second cycle of reading and present question/task.
Task: Underline three important facts about the topic. Using the writing map, write Supporting Details and explain the important facts in your own words.

Step 8: Provide time for discussion.
Review important facts about the topic, and stress that an informational text contains supporting details.

Step 9: Complete third cycle of reading and present question/task.
Question: Look back at the topic circled and the facts underlined. What is the main idea of this text? Using the writing map, write Main Idea and list the big idea you learned about this topic.

Step 10: Provide time for discussion.
Review what main ideas are and ensure that students understand what main ideas they learned from the text. Use the student-generated map as a scaffold for their expository essays on informational topics.

CLOSE READING FRAMEWORK

INTERMEDIATE EXPOSITORY WRITING

Step 1: Identify the text.
Choose a text that contains a clear examination of a nonfiction topic and incorporates text features.

Step 2: Determine purpose for reading.
To improve intermediate expository writing

Step 3: Choose a model.
Intermediate Expository Writing

Step 4: Decide how students will access texts.
Paired reading/Paired reading/Paired reading

Step 5: Complete first cycle of reading and present question/task.
Task: Circle the topic of the text. Underline key details. Draw arrows from main ideas to supporting details, then select a topic with which you are familiar. Write down the topic, main ideas, and supporting details in an expository essay map.

Step 6: Provide time for discussion.
Stress that main ideas and supporting details form the foundation for expository writing. Without them, the reader cannot learn about the topic.

Step 7: Complete second cycle of reading and present question/task.
Task: Put a star over linking words and phrases (e.g., first, second, third, for example, in contrast, in conclusion).
Add linking words and phrases between supporting details of expository essay map.

Step 8: Provide time for discussion.
Discuss how linking words and phrases provide a natural transition among main ideas and details.

Step 9: Complete third cycle of reading and present question/task.
Task/Question: Highlight any text features from the text (e.g., bold words, headings, graphs). Add into the expository essay map potential text features for your essay.

Step 10: Provide time for discussion.
Emphasize how text features help students to understand the text better. Review the text features from the model text, brainstorm additional features, and encourage students to share the text features they plan to integrate into their expository essay.
Use the student-generated map as a scaffold for their expository essays.

CLOSE READING FRAMEWORK

ADVANCED EXPOSITORY WRITING

Step 1:   Identify the text.
Choose a text that contains a clear examination of a nonfiction topic, incorporates text features, and offers a strong example of text structure.

Step 2:   Determine purpose for reading.
To improve advanced expository writing

Step 3:   Choose a model.
Advanced Expository Writing

Step 4:   Decide how students will access texts.
Paired reading/Paired reading/Paired reading

Step 5:   Complete first cycle of reading and present question/task.
Task: Circle the topic of the text. Underline main ideas. Draw arrows from main ideas to supporting details. Select a topic with which you are familiar. Write down the topic, main ideas, and supporting details in an expository essay map.

Step 6:   Provide time for discussion.
Stress that main ideas and supporting details form the foundation for expository writing. Without them, the reader cannot learn about the topic.

Step 7:   Complete second cycle of reading and present question/task.
Question: What is the text structure of this text? What text structure will you use for your own expository essay?

Step 8:   Provide time for discussion.
Refer back to the text to determine how students identified the text structure. Encourage students to share the text structure they will use for their expository essay. Probe to ensure that students are using the most appropriate text structure for their essay.

Step 9:   Complete third cycle of reading and present question/task.
Task: Highlight all of the vocabulary that is specialized for this topic. Brainstorm the specialized vocabulary that is appropriate to your topic.

Step 10: Provide time for discussion.
Discuss how specialized vocabulary provides the reader with a better understanding of the topic. Encourage students to share their own specialized vocabulary for their topic. Use the student-generated map as a scaffold for their expository essays.

CLOSE READING FRAMEWORK

COMPARING AND CONTRASTING CHARACTERS

Step 1: Identify the text.
Choose a text that includes two characters that can be easily compared/contrasted.

Step 2: Determine purpose for reading.
To improve compare/contrast essay writing skills

Step 3: Choose a model.
Comparing and Contrasting Characters

Step 4: Decide how students will access texts.
Paired reading/Paired reading/Paired reading

Step 5: Complete first cycle of reading and present question/task.
Task: Look at Character 1 and Character 2 in the story. Underline all of the words and phrases that the author uses to show how they are alike in blue.

Step 6: Provide time for discussion.
Focus the discussion first on what information students gleaned from their surface comprehension. Chart their answers.

Step 7: Complete second cycle of reading and present question/task.
Task: Look at Character 1. Circle in green all of the words and phrases that the author uses to show how this character is unique.

Step 8: Provide time for discussion.
Again, look at what is explicitly stated by the author. Chart their answers.

Step 9: Complete third cycle of reading and present question/task.
Task: Look at Character 2. Circle in red all of the words and phrases that the author uses to show how this character is unique.

Step 10: Provide time for discussion.
As before, chart their answers. Use the student text mark-ups as a scaffold for their essays, writing first about their similarities and then about each one's unique characteristics.

CLOSE READING FRAMEWORK

COMPARING AND CONTRASTING IDEAS OR EVENTS

Step 1: Identify the text.
Choose a text that includes two ideas or events that can be easily compared/contrasted.

Step 2: Determine purpose for reading.
To improve compare/contrast essay writing skills

Step 3: Choose a model.
Comparing and Contrasting Ideas or Events

Step 4: Decide how students will access texts.
Paired reading/Paired reading/Paired reading

Step 5: Complete first cycle of reading and present question/task.
Task: Look at Item 1 and Item 2 in the story. Underline all of the words and phrases that the author uses to show how they are alike in blue. Also, write in the margins any other similarities that you can infer from the text.

Step 6: Provide time for discussion.
Focus the discussion first on what information students gleaned from their surface comprehension. Then, ask them what similarities they inferred, requiring them to refer to the text to support their conclusions. Chart their answers.

Step 7: Complete second cycle of reading and present question/task.
Task: Look at Item 1. Circle in green all of the words and phrases that the author uses to show how this character is unique. Also, write in the margins any other differences that you can infer from the text.

Step 8: Provide time for discussion.
Again, look first at the literal comprehension and then at the inferential comprehension responses. Chart their answers.

Step 9: Complete third cycle of reading and present question/task.
Task: Look at Item 2. Circle in red all of the words and phrases that the author uses to show how this character is unique. Also, write in the margins any other differences that you can infer from the text.

Step 10: Provide time for discussion.
As before, look first at the literal comprehension and then at the inferential comprehension responses. Chart their answers. Use the student text mark-ups and annotations as a scaffold for their essays, writing first about their similarities and then about each one's unique characteristics.

CLOSE READING FRAMEWORK

BEGINNING OPINION ESSAYS

Step 1: Identify the text.
Choose a text that emphasizes an opinion.

Step 2: Determine purpose for reading.
To improve opinion writing skills

Step 3: Choose a model.
Beginning Opinion Essays

Step 4: Decide how students will access texts.
Paired reading/Paired reading/Paired reading

Step 5: Complete first cycle of reading and present question/task.
Task/Question: Circle the opinion that the author expresses in the story. What is your opinion about this topic? Is it the same or different? Write down your opinion.

Step 6: Provide time for discussion.
Review the opinion from the text. Ask students what opinion they hold.

Step 7: Complete second cycle of reading and present question/task.
Task/Question: Underline the reasons the author gives for the opinion. What reasons do you have for your opinion? Write down three reasons for your opinion.

Step 8: Provide time for discussion.
Emphasize that everyone has opinions, but good writers explain to the reader what reasons support their opinion. Ask students to share their reasons, ensuring that the reasons are rational and logical.

Step 9: Complete third cycle of reading and present question/task.
Task: Draw a box around the part of the text that shows the conclusion statement for the opinion. Write down a sentence that wraps up your opinion.

Step 10: Provide time for discussion.
Emphasize that all text needs a conclusion so that the reader is not just left to wonder how the text ends. Encourage students to share their conclusions. Use the student-generated writing maps as a scaffold for their essays.

CLOSE READING FRAMEWORK

ADVANCED OPINION ESSAYS

Step 1:   Identify the text.
Choose a text that emphasizes an opinion.

Step 2:   Determine purpose for reading.
To improve opinion writing skills

Step 3:   Choose a model.
Advanced Opinion Essays

Step 4:   Decide how students will access texts.
Paired reading/Paired reading/Paired reading

Step 5:   Complete first cycle of reading and present question/task.
Task/Question: Circle the opinion that the author expresses in the story. What is your opinion about this topic? Is it the same or different? Write down your opinion.

Step 6:   Provide time for discussion.
Review the opinion from the book. Ask students what opinion they hold.

Step 7:   Complete second cycle of reading and present question/task.
Task/Question: Underline the reasons the author gives for the opinion. Draw arrows from the reasons to supporting details. What reasons do you have for your opinion? Write down three reasons for your opinion and two to three supporting facts.

Step 8:   Provide time for discussion.
Emphasize that everyone has opinions, but good writers explain to the reader what reasons support the opinion and provide reasoning for their opinion. Ask students to share their reasons and support, ensuring that the reasons and support are rational and logical.

Step 9: Complete third cycle of reading and present question/task.
Question: Are the reasons in the text in a logical order?
Are they most important to least important? Are they
from least important to most important? Does the order
make sense to you as the reader? Number your reasons in
a logical order.

Step 10: Provide time for discussion.
Discuss how the order of reasons can strengthen or
weaken an opinion. Encourage students to share their
own order and their rationale for the placement. Use
the student-generated writing maps as a scaffold
for their essays.

ARGUMENTATIVE WRITING ESSAY

Step 1: Identify the text.
Choose a text that contains a well-written argument.

Step 2: Determine purpose for reading.
To improve argumentative writing skills

Step 3: Choose a model.
Argument Writing Essay

Step 4: Decide how students will access texts.
Paired reading/Paired reading/Paired reading

Step 5: Complete first cycle of reading and present question/task.
Task/Question: Underline the argument of the text.
Do you agree or disagree? Write down your argument
in one sentence.

CLOSE READING FRAMEWORK

Step 6: Provide time for discussion.
Discuss the author's argument. Encourage students to share their own argument positions.

Step 7: Complete second cycle of reading and present question/task.
Task/Question: Draw a box around reasons and circle the evidence to support the argument. What evidence do you have to support your own claim?

Step 8: Provide time for discussion.
Stress that arguments must have credible evidence. Review the text to determine if the author's reasons and evidence were credible. Ask student to share their own reasons and evidence and evaluate if it is credible.

Step 9: Complete third cycle of reading and present question/task.
Task/Question: Circle examples of the author recognizing an alternative viewpoint. How can you acknowledge an alternative viewpoint as a means to strengthen your argument?

Step 10: Provide time for discussion.
Reinforce that argumentative writing is an objective style of writing necessitating reasons, evidence, and acknowledging alternative viewpoints. Use the student-generated discussions as a scaffold for their essays.

CLOSE READING FRAMEWORK

TEXT SUMMARIES

Step 1: Identify the text.
Choose a succinct text that has clear main ideas.

Step 2: Determine purpose for reading.
To improve summarization of skills

Step 3: Choose a model.
Text Summaries

Step 4: Decide how students will access texts.
Independent reading/Independent reading/Independent reading

Step 5: Complete first cycle of reading and present question/task.
Question/Task: If you had to summarize the text for a friend who had never read this text, which information would not be important to share with him/her? Cross out all insignificant information.

Step 6: Provide time for discussion.
Discuss what information from the text is insignificant and why it is unimportant to the main ideas of the text.

Step 7: Complete second cycle of reading and present question/task.
Question/Task: What is the main idea(s) of this text?
Circle the main idea(s).

Step 8: Provide time for discussion.
Review the main idea(s) of the text and how a reader can identify them as central to the text.

Step 9: Complete third cycle of reading and present question/task.
Question/Task: Look at the remaining sentences. These should be supporting details for your main idea(s). Underline the supporting details and draw an arrow to the main idea which they support.

Step 10: Provide time for discussion.
Ensure that the supporting details align to the correct main idea(s). Review the text, using only the main idea(s) and supporting details of the text. Have students work in pairs to summarize the text using their mark-ups as a guide. Then, ask pairs to share their oral summaries. Use the text mark-ups to create a text summary.

CLOSE READING FRAMEWORK

POETRY

Step 1: Identify the text.
Choose a text that illustrates a particular poetic form.

Step 2: Determine purpose for reading.
To improve poetry writing skills

Step 3: Choose a model.
Poetry

Step 4: Decide how students will access texts.
Shared reading/Small-group reading/Independent reading

Step 5: Complete first cycle of reading and present question/task.
Question: How is this poem a good example of ___ (haiku, couplet, limerick, free verse, etc.)? How do you know? (NOTE: Give characteristics of poetic form being read prior to the first reading cycle.)

Step 6: Provide time for discussion.
Review the poetic form characteristics being read and how those characteristics are reflected in the model poem.

Step 7: Complete second cycle of reading and present question/task.
Question: What is the theme of the poem? What theme would you like your poem to share?

Step 8: Provide time for discussion.
Remind students that the theme of the poem reflects the text's lesson.

Step 9: Complete third cycle of reading and present question/task.
Question: What is the mood of the poem (e.g., joyous, sad, serious, funny)? In what mood will you write your poem?

Step 10: Provide time for discussion.
Discuss what the mood of the poem is, asking students to provide clues from the text to support their answers. Then, inquire about the mood of the student-generated poems and how they will create mood in their work. Use the student-generated discussions as a scaffold for their poetry.

CLOSE READING FRAMEWORK

GENRE WRITING

Step 1: Identify the text.
Choose a text that illustrates a particular genre.

Step 2: Determine purpose for reading.
To improve writing skills in specific literacy genre

Step 3: Choose a model.
Genre Writing

Step 4: Decide how students will access texts.
Small-group reading/Paired reading/Independent reading

Step 5: Complete first cycle of reading and present question/task.
Question: Who are the characters in this story? What is the setting? How are the setting and these characters common to this genre? Use details from the text to support your thinking.

Step 6: Provide time for discussion.
Review the story, drawing student attention to the characters and setting and their relationship to the genre. For example, characters in historical fiction behave realistically and may be real people who lived in the past or represent fictional characters common to that time period and place.

Step 7: Complete second cycle of reading and present question/task.
Question: What is the problem in this story? How is this problem common to this genre? Use details from the text to support your thinking.

Step 8: Provide time for discussion.
Focus on the problem and how it characterizes the genre. For example, the problem in historical fiction must be relevant to that time period and place.

Step 9: Complete third cycle of reading and present question/task.
Question: What is the solution in this story? How is this solution common to this genre? Use details from the text to support your thinking.

Step 10: Provide time for discussion.
Emphasize that the solution must be one that makes sense in that time period and place. For example, the solution in a historical fiction story must be resolved in a way that is probable and relevant during that time. Use the student-generated discussions as a scaffold for their genre-specific writing.

Chapter Summary

Of the three R's in classrooms—reading, writing, and arithmetic—reading and math have dominated in this era of student achievement, standardized testing, and teacher accountability. Writing, unfortunately, has been neglected, deemed insignificant specifically in the urgency for students to become good readers. In the face of ongoing calls for the need of writing instruction to take its place in literacy instruction, students still under-perform in writing skills with approximately 75 percent of students in grades 4–12 described as poor writers. This trend continues in postsecondary schools as well as in the job market.

Even with decades of research supporting the benefits of the reading–writing connection, schools still treat these two academic domains as separate fields of study. This inattention manifests itself in not just writing achievement but also in the reading achievement of students. If students are to learn, they must be able to express their understanding through their own writing. It is those students who cannot demonstrate their thinking on the written page or on the screen of a digital device who struggle academically.

Close writes gather the research base of the reading–writing connection to scaffold students in both their reading and, more specifically, in their writing development. Following the same ten-step framework as close reading, close writes ask students to re-read a short piece of text for the purpose of deeper understanding of the text's meaning. Using that knowledge as well as the tangible text mark-ups and discussion that ensue about the writing of the passage, students write their own creative piece. This strategy will accelerate writing skill development in a supportive instructional environment that ensures that all students are equipped with the same building blocks to become the writers they need to be to meet the demands of this technological world.

Book Study

Reflection Questions

Chapter 8: Close Writes as a Springboard into Student-Generated Writing

1. Should there be a writing revolution? What evidence do you see in your classroom, your school, your community, and the world that suggests such a revolution is necessary?

2. Do you emphasize the reading–writing connection in your classroom, your school? How?

3. Do you believe that how we approach writing instruction will change in the coming years? Why?

4. *TASK:* Focus on an upcoming writing assignment in your classroom. Develop a close write lesson to prepare your students to generate their own original piece.

REFERENCES

Achieve the Core. (2013). *Text complexity collection.* Retrieved from www.corestandards.org/ELA-Literacy

ACT, Inc. (2006). *Reading between the lines: What the ACT reveals about college readiness in reading.* Retrieved from www.act.org/research/policymakers/pdf/reading_report.pdf

Adler, M. J. (1940). *How to read a book: The art of getting a liberal education.* New York, NY: Simon & Schuster.

Adler, M. J. (1941, July 6). How to mark a book. *The Saturday Literature Review,* pp. 11–12.

Adler, M. J., & Van Doren, C. L. (1972). *How to read a book: The classic guide to intelligent reading.* New York, NY: Simon & Schuster.

Akhondi, M., Malayeri, F. A., & Samad, A. A. (2011). How to teach expository text structure to facilitate reading comprehension. *The Reading Teacher, 64*(5), 368–372.

Allington, R. L. (2001). *What really matters for struggling readers.* New York, NY: Addison-Wesley.

American Diploma Project. (2004). *Ready or not: Creating a high school diploma that counts.* Washington, DC: Achieve.

Anderson, T. H., & Armbruster, B. B. (1984). *Producing "considerate" expository text: Or easy reading is damned hard writing* (Reading Education Report No. 46). Champaign, IL: University of Illinois at Urbana-Champaign. Retrieved from www.ideals.illinois.edu/bitstream/handle/2142/17473/ctrstreadeducrepv01984i00046_opt.pdf?sequence=1

Applebee, A. N., & Langer, J. A. (2006). *The state of writing instruction in America's schools: What existing data tell us.* Albany, NY: Center on English Learning & Achievement, University at Albany, State University of New York.

Bamberg, B. (1983). Coherence and cohesion: What are they and how are they achieved? *College Composition and Communication, 34*(4), 417–429.

Biancarosa, G., & Snow, C. E. (2004). *Reading next—A vision for action and research in middle and high school literacy: A report to Carnegie Corporation of New York.* Washington, DC: Alliance for Excellent Education.

Bloom, B. S. (Ed.). (1956). *Taxonomy of educational objectives: Book 1 cognitive domain.* White Plains, NY: Longman.

Bluestein, N. A. (2010). Unlocking text features for determining importance in expository text: A strategy for struggling readers. *The Reading Teacher, 63*(7), 597–600. doi: 10.1598/RT.63.7.7

Brown, S., & Kappes, L. (2012). *Implementing the common core state standards: A primer on "close reading" of text.* Washington, DC: The Aspen Institute.

Brozo, W. G. (2002). *To be a boy, to be a reader: Engaging teen and pre-teen boys in active literacy.* Newark, DE: International Reading Association.

Brummet, B. S. (2010). *Techniques of close reading.* Thousand Oaks, CA: Sage Publications.

Burnett, C. (2013). Investigating pupils' interactions around digital texts: A spatial perspective on the "classroom-ness" of digital literacy practices in schools. *Educational Review,* 3–13. Retrieved from ww.tandfonline.com/doi/citedby/10.1080/00131911.2013.768959#tabModule

Calkins, L., Ehrenworth, M., & Lehman, C. (2012). *Pathways to the common core: Accelerating achievement.* Portsmouth, NH: Heinemann.

Cambria, J., & Gutherie, J. T. (2010). Motivating and engaging students in reading. *The NERA Journal, 46*(1), 16–29.

Cohn, M. M. & Kottkamp, R. B. (1993). *Teachers: The missing voice in education.* Albany, NY: State University of New York Press.

Coiro, J. (2011). Talking about reading as thinking: Modeling the hidden complexities of online reading comprehension. *Theory Into Practice, 50,* 107–115. doi: 10.1080/00405841.2011.558435

Coiro, J., & Fogleman, J. (2011). Using websites wisely. *Educational Leadership, 68*(5), 34–38.

Coleman, D. (2011). *David Coleman: Common core: Summer 2011*. [Audio podcast]. Retrieved from www.youtube.com/watch?v=aTCiQVC pdQc&feature=youtu.be

Cooper, T. C. (1998). Teaching idioms. *Foreign Language Annals, (31)*2, 255–266.

Cowan, J., & Kessler, J. (2013, October 20). The middle class gets wise. *The New York Times, p. SR4.*

Crowe, M., & Stanford, P. (2010). Questioning for quality. *Phi Delta Gamma Bulletin, 76*(4), 36–41, 44.

Deloitte Development LLC. (2011). *Boiling point? The skills gap in U.S. manufacturing*. Retrieved from www.themanufacturinginstitute. org/~/media/A07730B2A798437D98501E798C2E13AA.ashx

Duke, N. K. (2000). 3.6 minutes per day: The scarcity of informational texts in first grade. *Reading Research Quarterly, 35,* 202–224.

Empson, R. (1947). *Seven types of ambiguity*. New York, NY: New Directions.

Fisher, D., & Frey, N. (2013). Close reading in elementary schools. *The Reading Teacher, 66*(3), 179–188.

Fisher, D., Frey, N., & Lapp, D. (2012). *Text complexity: Raising rigor in reading*. Newark, DE: International Reading Association.

Fletcher, R., & Portalupi, J. (1998). *Craft lessons: Teaching writing k-8.* Portland, ME: Stenhouse Publishers.

Flippo, R. F., & Caverly, D. C. (2009). *Handbook of college reading and study strategy research.* (2nd ed). New York, NY: Taylor & Francis.

Flowers, T. A., & Flowers, L. A. (2009). Nonfiction in the early grades: Making reading and writing relevant for all students. *Journal for the Liberal Arts and Sciences, 13*(2), 40–50.

Gewertz, C. (2013, October 9). Global study identifies promising practices in top-scoring nations. *Education Week, p. 9.*

Gibson, S. A. (2008). An effective framework for primary-grade writing instruction. *The Reading Teacher, 62*(4), 324–334.

Gill, S. R. (2009). What teachers need to know about the "new" nonfiction. *The Reading Teacher, 63*(4), 260–267.

Good, T. L., & Brophy, J. (2000). *Looking in classrooms.* (8th ed). New York, NY: Longman.

Goodman, K. S. (1989). Whole-language research: Foundations and development. *The Elementary School Journal, 90*(2), 207–221.

Gorman, M. J. (2009). *Elements of biblical exegesis: A basic guide for students and ministers.* Peabody, MA: Hendrickson Publishers.

Graham, S., & Hebert, M. A. (2010). *Writing to read: Evidence for how writing can improve reading. A Carnegie Corporation Time to Act Report.* Washington, DC: Alliance for Excellent Education.

Graham, S., Bollinger, A., Booth Olson, C., D'Aoust, C., MacArthur, C., McCutchen, D., & Olinghouse, N. (2012). *Teaching elementary school students to be effective writers: A practical guide.* (NCEE 2012–4058). Washington, DC: National Center for Education Evaluation and Regional Assistance, Institute of Education Sciences, U. S. Department of Education. Retrieved from http:// ies.ed.gov/ncee/wwc/publications_reviews.aspx#pubsearch

Gray, L., Thomas, N., & Lewis, L. (2010). *Teachers' use of educational technology in U.S. public schools: 2009 (NCES 2010–040).* Washington, DC: National Center for Education Statistics, Institute of Education Sciences, U. S. Department of Education.

Groen, D. H. (1996). Coherence. In T. Enos (Ed.). *Encyclopedia of rhetoric and composition: Communication from ancient times to the information age.* New York: NY: Taylor & Francis.

Gutteridge, D. (2000). *Teaching English: Theory and practice from kindergarten to grade twelve.* Toronto, Ontario: James Lorimer & Company.

Harris, R. (2010, November 22). *Evaluating internet research sources.* Retrieved from www.virtualsalt.com/evalu8it.htm

Harris, T. L., & Hodges, R. E. (Eds.). (1995). *The literacy dictionary: The vocabulary of reading and writing.* Newark, DE: International Reading Association.

Hess, K., & Hervey, S. (2011). *Tools for examining text complexity.* Retrieved from www.nciea.org/publication_PDFs/Updated% 20toolkit-text%20complexity_KH12.pdf

Hiebert, E. H. (2011). *Using multiple sources of information in establishing text complexity* (Reading Research Report No. 11.03). Santa Cruz, CA: TextProject & University of California, Santa Cruz. Retrieved from textproject.org/research/reading-research-reports/a-case-for-using-multiple-sources-of-information-in-establishing-text-complexity

Hiebert, E. H. (2012, June 21). *Teaching complex text: Why look at word frequency.* [Web log message] Retrieved from http://textproject. org/frankly-freddy/teaching-complex-text-why-look-at-word-frequency

Hiebert, E. H. (2013). Text complexity and English learners—Building vocabulary. *Text Issues, 2*(1), 1–6.

Juel, D. (1998). *Messianic exegesis: Christological interpretation of the old testament in early Christianity.* Minneapolis, MN: Fortress Press.

Karchmer-Klein, R., & Shinas, V. H. (2012). Guiding principles for supporting new literacies in your classroom. *The Reading Teacher, 65*(5), 288–293. doi: 10.1002/TRTR.01044

Katusic, S. K., Colligan, R. C., Weaver, A. L., & Barbaresi, W. J. (2009). The forgotten learning ability: Epidemiology of written-language disorder in a population-based cohort (1976–1982), Rochester, Minnesota. *Pediatrics, 123*(5), 1306–1313.

Krashen, S D. (1993). *The power of reading: Insights from the research.* Portsmouth, NH: Heinemann.

Kühnen, U., van Egmond, M. C., Haber, F., Kuschel, S., Özelsel, A., Rossi, A. L., & Spivak, Y. (2012). Challenge me! Communicating in multicultural classrooms. *Social Psychology of Education, 15*(1), 59–76.

Langer, J. A., & Flihan, S. (2000). Writing and reading relationships. In R. Indrisano and J. R. Squire (Eds.). *Perspectives on writing: Research, theory, and practice.* Newark, DE: International Reading Association.

Leu, D. J., Jr., Kinzer, C. K., Coiro, J. L., & Cammack, D. W. (2004). Toward a theory of new literacies emerging from the internet and other information and communication technologies. In R. B. Ruddell, & N. J. Unrau (Eds.). *Theoretical models and processes of reading.* (5th edn, pp. 1570–1613). Newark, DC: International Reading Association.

Leu, D. J., McVerry, J. G., O'Bryne, W. I., Kiili, C., Zawilinski, L., Everett-Cacopardo, H., Kennedy, C., & Forzani, E. (2011). The new literacies of online reading comprehension: Expanding the literacy and learning curriculum. *Journal of Adolescent and Adult Literacy, 55*(1), 5–14. doi: 10.1598/JAAL.55.1.1

Levin, T., & Long, R. (1981). *Effective instruction*. Washington, D.C.: ASCD.

Mangen, A. (2008). Hypertext fiction reading: Haptics and immersion. *Journal of Research in Reading, 31*(4), 409–419.

Marzano, R. J. (2004). *Building background knowledge for academic achievement*. Alexandria, VA: Association for Supervision and Curriculum Development.

Morgan, D. N., & Rasinski, T. V. (2012). The power and potential of primary sources. *The Reading Teacher, 65*(8), 584–594. doi: 10.1002/TRTR.01086

National Commission on Writing for America's Families, Schools, and Colleges. (2003). *The neglected "r": The need for a writing revolution*. New York, NY: College Entrance Examination Board.

National Commission on Writing for America's Families, Schools, and Colleges. (2004). *Writing: A ticket to work . . . or a ticket out: A survey of business leaders*. New York, NY: College Entrance Examination Board.

National Governors Association Center for Best Practices and Council of Chief State School Officers. (2010). *Common core state standards for English language arts and literacy in history/social studies, science, and technical subjects. Appendix A: Research supporting key elements of the standards and glossary of key terms*. Washington, DC: Authors. Retrieved from www.corestandards.org/ELA-Literacy

Nelson, N., & Calfee, R. C. (Eds.). (1998). *The reading-writing connection: 97th yearbook of the national society for the study of education*. Chicago, IL: University of Chicago Press.

North Central Regional Educational Laborator and the Metiri Group. (2003). *enGauge 21st century skills: Literacy in the digital age*. Retrieved from http://pict.sdsu.edu/engauge21st.pdf

Parsad, B., & Jones, J. (2005). *Internet access in U. S. public schools and classrooms: 1994–2003*. (NCES 2005–015). U. S. Department of Education. Washington, DC: National Center for Education Statistics.

Partnership for Assessment of Readiness for College and Careers. (2011). *PARCC model content frameworks: English language arts/ literacy grades 3–11*. Retrieved from www.parcconline.org/sites/parcc/files/PARCCMCFELALiteracyAugust2012_FINAL.pdf

Paulson, E. J., & Armstrong, S. L. (2010). Situating reader stance within and beyond the efferent-aesthetic continuum. *Literacy Research and Instruction, 49*, 86–97. doi: 10.1080/19388070902736821

Pollio, H. R., Barlow, J. M., Fine, H. J., & Pollio, M. R. (1977). *Psychology and the poetics of growth: Figurative language in psychology, psychotherapy, and education.* Hillsdale, NJ: Lawrence Erlbaum Associates.

Ransom, J. C. (1941). *The new criticism.* Norfolk, CT: New Directions.

Richards, I. A. (1929). *Practical criticism: A study of literary judgment.* London: Kegan Paul, Trench, Trubner, & Co.

Rosenblatt, L. M. (1938). *Literature as exploration.* New York, NY: D. Appleton-Century.

Rosenblatt, L. M. (1978). *The reader, the text, the poem: The Transactional Theory of the literary work.* Carbondale, IL: Southern Illinois University Press.

Routman, R. (2000). *Conversations: Strategies for teaching, learning, and evaluation.* Portsmouth, NH: Heinemann.

Shanahan, T. (2006). Relations among oral language, reading, and writing development. In C. MacArthur, S. Graham, & J. Fitzgerald (Eds.). *Handbook of Writing Research.* (pp. 171–184). New York, NY: The Guildford Press.

Shanahan, T. (2012, June 18). Re: *What is close reading?* [Web log message] Retrieved from www.shanahanonliteracy.com/2012/06/what-is-close-reading.html

Snow, C. E., Burns, M. S., & Griffin, P. (1998). *Preventing reading difficulties in young children.* Washington, DC: National Academy Press.

Spolsky, E. (1990). *The uses of adversity: Failure and accommodation in reader response.* Cranbury, NJ: Associated University Presses.

Stevens, K. C. (1980). The effect of background knowledge on the reading comprehension of ninth graders. *Journal of Reading Behavior, 12*(2), 151–154.

Swanson, C. B. (2010). U.S. graduation rate continues decline. *Education Week, 29*(34), 22–23, 30.

Taylor, M. (Ed.). (2007). *Whole language teaching, whole hearted practice: Looking back, looking forward.* New York, NY: Peter Lang Publishing Inc.

Troia, G. A., & Olinghouse, N. G. (2013). The Common Core State Standards and evidence-based educational practices: The case of writing. *School Psychology Review, 42*(3), 343–357.

Tyre, P. (2012, September 19). The writing revolution. *The Atlantic, 310*(3), 96–101.

U. S. Department of Education (USDOE). (1980). *What works: Research about teaching and learning.* Washington, D.C.: USDOE.

Webb, N. L. (1997a). *Criteria for alignment of expectations and assessments in mathematics and science education.* Council of Chief State School Officers and National Institute for Science Education Research Monograph No. 8. Madison, WI: University of Wisconsin, Wisconsin Center for Education Research.

Webb, N. L. (1997b, January). *Determining alignment of expectations and assessments in mathematics and science education.* NISE Issue Brief. Madison, WI: National Institute for Science Education, UW–Madison.

Webb, N. L. (1999). *Alignment of science and mathematics standards and assessment in four states.* Council of Chief State School Officers and National Institute for Science Education Research Monograph No. 18. Madison, WI: University of Wisconsin, Wisconsin Center for Education Research.

Williams, T. L. (2009). A framework for nonfiction in the elementary grades. *Literacy Research and Instruction, 48*(3), 247–263.

Yopp, R. H., & Yopp, H. K. (2012). Children's limited and narrow exposure to informational text. *The Reading Teacher, 65*(7), 480–490.